the milk cotton *collection*

15 designs by Marie Wallin using Rowan Milk Cotton DK & Fine Milk Cotton

Thomasina

Harmonie

Camellia

Cicilia

Lenora

Magda

Caitlyn

Wilhemia Cardi

Bailey

Maryjo

Abigail

Gerty

Jocelynn

Wilhemia Jumper

Eadie

gallery

YARN

	S	M	L	XL	XXL	
To fit bust	81-86	91-97	102-107	112-117	122-127	cm
	32-34	36-38	40-42	44-46	48-50	in
Rowan Milk Cotton DK						
	11	11	12	13	14	x 50gm

(photographed in Cream Soda 095)

HOOKS – 3.50mm (no 9) (US E4) crochet hook

BUTTONS – 4 x BN1152

TENSION – 19 sts and 21 rows to 10 cm measured over dc fabric using 3.50mm (US E4) hook

CROCHET ABBREVIATIONS

ch = chain; **ss** = slip stitch; **dc** = double crochet; **htr** = half treble; **tr** = treble; **dc2tog** = (insert hook as indicated, yoh and draw loop through) twice, yoh and draw through all 3 loops; **tr3tog** = (yoh and insert hook as indicated, yoh and draw loop through, yoh and draw through 2 loops) 3 times, yoh and draw through all 4 loops; **sp(s)** = space(s); **yoh** = yarn over hook.

LOWER BODY FRILL

Using 3.50mm (US E4) hook, make 160 [180: 200: 224: 252] ch.
Row 1 (WS): 1 dc into 2nd ch from hook, 1 dc into each ch to end, turn. 159 [179: 199: 223: 251] sts.
Row 2: 1 ch (does NOT count as st), 1 dc into each of first 7 [4: 9: 11: 13] dc, 2 dc into next dc, (1 dc into each of next 11 [6: 4: 3: 3] dc, 2 dc into next dc, 1 dc into each of next 11 [5: 3: 3: 3] dc, 2 dc into next dc) 6 [13: 20: 25: 28] times, 1 dc into each of last 7 [5: 9: 11: 13] dc, turn. 172 [206: 240: 274: 308] sts.
Row 3: 1 ch (does NOT count as st), 1 dc into each dc to end, turn.
Rows 4 to 9: As row 3.
Row 10 (RS): 1 ch (does NOT count as st), 1 dc into each of first 8 dc, ★4 ch, miss 3 dc★★, 1 dc into each of next 14 dc, rep from ★ to end, ending last rep at ★★, 1 dc into each of last 8 dc, turn. 10 [12: 14: 16: 18] patt reps.
Row 11: 3 ch (counts as first htr and 1 ch), miss first 2 dc, ★1 dc into each of next 3 dc, 1 ch, miss 3 dc, (1 tr and 1 ch) 6 times into next ch sp, miss 3 dc, 1 dc into each of next 3 dc★★, 3 ch, miss 2 dc, rep from ★ to end, ending last rep at ★★, 1 ch, miss 1 dc, 1 htr into last dc, turn.
Row 12: 1 ch (does NOT count as st), 1 dc into first htr, 2 ch, miss (1 ch and 3 dc), ★(tr3tog into next ch sp, 2 ch) 7 times★★, 1 dc into next ch sp, 2 ch, rep from ★ to end, ending last rep at ★★, 1 dc into 2nd of 3 ch at beg of previous row, turn.
Row 13: 1 ch (does NOT count as st), 1 dc into first dc, ★2 dc into next ch sp, 1 dc into next tr3tog, 2 dc into next ch sp, (3 ch, miss 1 tr3tog, 2 dc into next ch sp) twice, 5 ch, miss 1 tr3tog, (2 dc into next ch sp, 3 ch, miss 1 tr3tog) twice, 2 dc into next ch sp, 1 dc into next tr3tog, 2 dc into next ch sp★★, miss 1 dc, rep from ★ to end, ending last rep at ★★, 1 dc into last dc.
Fasten off.

UPPER BODY FRILL

Work as given for lower frill to end of row 3.
Complete as given for lower frill from row 10 to end.

BODY (worked in one piece to armholes)

Lay WS of upper body frill against RS of lower body frill so that foundation ch edges match.
With RS of upper frill facing and using 3.50mm (US E4) hook, attach yarn at one end of frill foundation ch edges and work 1 row of dc across foundation ch edges of frills, working each dc through each foundation ch of upper and lower frills so that edges are joined tog, turn. 159 [179: 199: 223: 251] sts.
Next row (WS): 4 ch (counts as first tr and 1 ch), miss first 2 dc, 1 tr into next dc, ★1 ch, miss 1 dc, 1 tr into next dc, rep from ★ to end, turn.
Next row: 4 ch (counts as first tr and 1 ch), miss (1 tr and 1 ch) at end of previous row, 1 tr into next tr, ★1 ch, miss 1 ch, 1 tr into next tr, rep from ★ to end, working tr at end of last rep into 3rd of 4 ch at beg of previous row, turn.
Next row: 1 ch (does NOT count as st), 1 dc into each tr and ch sp to end, working last dc into 3rd of 4 ch at beg of previous row, turn. 159 [179: 199: 223: 251] sts.
Next row: 1 ch (does NOT count as st), 1 dc into each dc to end, turn. Last row forms dc fabric.
Work in dc fabric for a further 5 rows, ending with RS facing for next row.
Next row (inc) (RS): 1 ch (does NOT count as st), 1 dc into each of first 38 [43: 48: 54: 61] dc, 2 dc into each of next 2 dc, 1 dc into each of next 79 [89: 99: 111: 125] dc, 2 dc into each of next 2 dc, 1 dc into each of last 38 [43: 48: 54: 61] dc, turn. 163 [183: 203: 227: 255] sts.
Work 13 rows.
Next row (inc) (RS): 1 ch (does NOT count as st), 1 dc into each of first 39 [44: 49: 55: 62] dc, 2 dc into each of next 2 dc, 1 dc into each of next 81 [91: 101: 113: 127] dc, 2 dc into each of next 2 dc, 1 dc into each of last 39 [44: 49: 55: 62] dc, turn. 167 [187: 207: 231: 259] sts.
Cont in dc fabric until body meas 22 [23: 24: 25: 26] cm from lower edge of lower frill, ending with RS facing for next row.
Shape front slopes
Next row (RS): 1 ch (does NOT count as st), dc2tog over first 2 dc – 1 st decreased, 1 dc into each dc to last 2 dc, dc2tog over last 2 dc – 1 st decreased, turn. 165 [185: 205: 229: 257] sts.
Working all decreases as set by last row, dec 1 st at each end of 2nd and foll 7 [6: 7: 6: 7] alt rows. 149 [171: 189: 215: 241] sts.
Work 1 [3: 1: 3: 1] rows, ending with RS facing for next row.
Divide for armholes and shape right front
Next row (RS): 1 ch (does NOT count as st), (dc2tog over first 2 dc) 0 [1: 0: 1: 0] times, 1 dc into each of next 28 [31: 36: 40: 47] dc and turn, leaving rem sts unworked.
Work on this set of 28 [32: 36: 41: 47] sts only for right front.
Dec 1 st armhole edge of next 4 [6: 8: 10: 12] rows, then on foll 4 [4: 3: 3: 4] alt rows **and at same time** dec 1 st at front slope edge of 2nd [4th:

2nd: 4th: 2nd] and 2 [2: 3: 3: 4] foll 4th rows. 17 [19: 21: 24: 26] sts.
Dec 1 st at front slope edge **only** on 2nd [2nd: 4th: 4th: 2nd] and 5 foll 4th rows. 11 [13: 15: 18: 20] sts.
Cont straight until armhole meas 19 [20: 21: 22: 23] cm, ending with RS facing for next row.

Shape shoulder
Fasten off.

Shape back
Return to last complete row worked before dividing for armholes, miss next 8 [10: 12: 14: 16] dc, rejoin yarn to next dc, 1 ch (does NOT count as st), 1 dc into st where yarn was rejoined, 1 dc into each of next 76 [84: 92: 102: 114] dc and turn, leaving rem sts unworked.
Work on this set of 77 [85: 93: 103: 115] sts only for back.
Dec 1 st at each end of next 4 [6: 8: 10: 12] rows, then on foll 4 [4: 3: 3: 4] alt rows. 61 [65: 71: 77: 83] sts.
Cont straight until 4 rows less have been worked than on right front to shoulder fasten-off, ending with RS facing for next row.

Shape back neck
Next row (RS): 1 ch (does NOT count as st), 1 dc into each of next 14 [16: 18: 21: 23] dc and turn, leaving rem sts unworked.
Work on this set of 14 [16: 18: 21: 23] sts only for first side of neck.
Dec 1 st neck edge of next 3 rows, ending with RS facing for next row. 11 [13: 15: 18: 20] sts.

Shape shoulder
Fasten off.
Return to last complete row worked before shaping back neck, miss next 33 [33: 35: 35: 37] dc, rejoin yarn to next dc, 1 ch (does NOT count as st), 1 dc into st where yarn was rejoined, 1 dc into each of next 13 [15: 17: 20: 22] dc, turn.
Dec 1 st neck edge of next 3 rows, ending with RS facing for next row. 11 [13: 15: 18: 20] sts.

Shape shoulder
Fasten off.

Shape left front
Return to last complete row worked before dividing for armholes, miss next 8 [10: 12: 14: 16] dc, rejoin yarn to next dc, 1 ch (does NOT count as st), 1 dc into st where yarn was rejoined, 1 dc into each dc to last 0 [2: 0: 2: 0] dc, (dc2tog over last 2 dc) 0 [1: 0: 1: 0] times, turn.
28 [32: 36: 41: 47] sts.
Complete to match right front, reversing shapings.

LOWER SLEEVE FRILLS
Using 3.50mm (US E4) hook, make 50 [52: 54: 56: 58] ch.
Row 1 (WS): 1 dc into 2nd ch from hook, 1 dc into each ch to end, turn. 49 [51: 53: 55: 57] sts.
Row 2: 1 ch (does NOT count as st), 1 dc into each of first 4 [2: 2: 2: 1] dc, 2 dc into next dc, (1 dc into each of next
1 [1: 2: 2: 3] dc, 2 dc into next dc, 1 dc into each of next
1 [2: 2: 3: 4] dc, 2 dc into next dc) 10 [9: 8: 7: 6] times,
1 dc into each of last 4 [3: 2: 3: 1] dc, turn. 70 sts.
Row 3: 1 ch (does NOT count as st), 1 dc into each dc to end, turn.
Complete as given for lower body frill from row 4 to end, noting that there are 4 patt reps.

UPPER SLEEVE FRILLS
Work as given for lower sleeve frill to end of row 3.
Complete as given for lower body frill from row 10 to end, noting that there are 4 patt reps.

SLEEVES
Lay WS of upper sleeve frill against RS of lower sleeve frill so that foundation ch edges match.
With RS of upper frill facing and using 3.50mm (US E4) hook, attach yarn at one end of frill foundation ch edges and work 1 row of dc across foundation ch edges of frills, working each dc through each foundation ch of upper and lower frills so that edges are joined tog, turn. 49 [51: 53: 55: 57] sts.
Next row (WS): 4 ch (counts as first tr and 1 ch), miss first 2 dc, 1 tr into next dc, *1 ch, miss 1 dc, 1 tr into next dc, rep from * to end, turn.
Next row: 4 ch (counts as first tr and 1 ch), miss (1 tr and 1 ch) at end of previous row, 1 tr into next tr, *1 ch, miss 1 ch, 1 tr into next tr, rep from * to end, working tr at end of last rep into 3rd of 4 ch at beg of previous row, turn.
Next row: 1 ch (does NOT count as st), 1 dc into each tr and ch sp to end, working last dc into 3rd of 4 ch at beg of previous row, turn.
49 [51: 53: 55: 57] sts.
This row sets dc fabric.
Next row: 1 ch (does NOT count as st), 2 dc into first dc − 1 st increased, 1 dc into each dc to last dc, 2 dc into last dc − 1 st increased, turn.
Working all increases as set by last row, inc 1 st at each end of 2nd and foll 3 [4: 5: 7: 9] alt rows, then on 3 [3: 3: 2: 1] foll 4th rows. 65 [69: 73: 77: 81] sts.
Cont straight until sleeve meas 26 [27: 28: 28: 28] cm from lower edge of lower frill, ending with RS facing for next row.

Shape top
Next row (RS): ss across and into 5th [6th: 7th: 8th: 9th] dc, 1 ch (does NOT count as st), 1 dc into same place as last ss,
1 dc into each dc to last 4 [5: 6: 7: 8] dc and turn, leaving rem sts unworked. 57 [59: 61: 63: 65] sts.
Dec 1 st at each end of next 21 [22: 23: 24: 25] rows. 15 sts.
Fasten off.

MAKING UP
Press as described on the information page.
Join both shoulder seams using back stitch, or mattress stitch if preferred.

Front band
With RS facing and using 3.50mm (US E4) hook, attach yarn at base of right front opening edge, 1 ch (does NOT count as st), work 1 row of dc evenly up entire right front opening edge, around back neck, then down entire left front opening edge to base of left front opening edge, turn.
Mark positions for 4 buttonholes along right front opening edge − first to come 3 cm up from base of right front opening edge, last to come just below beg of front slope shaping, and rem 2 buttonholes evenly spaced between.
Next row: 1 ch (does NOT count as st), 1 dc into each dc to end, making buttonholes to correspond with positions marked by replacing (1 dc into each of next 2 dc) with (2 ch, miss 2 dc), turn.
Next row: 1 ch (does NOT count as st), 1 dc into each dc to end, working 2 dc into each buttonhole ch sp.
Fasten off.
See information page for finishing instructions, setting in sleeves using the set-in method.

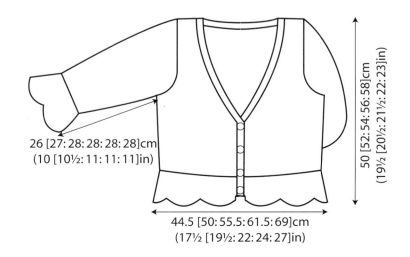

26 [27: 28: 28: 28: 28]cm
(10 [10½: 11: 11: 11]in)

50 [52:54:56:58]cm
(19½ [20½: 21½: 22:23]in)

44.5 [50:55.5:61.5:69]cm
(17½ [19½: 22: 24: 27]in)

YARN

			8	10	12	14	16	18		
To fit bust			81	86	91	97	102	107		cm
			32	34	36	38	40	42		in
Rowan Fine Milk Cotton										
A Liquorice	499		2	2	3	3	3	3	x	50gm
B Water Bomb	498		4	4	5	5	5	5	x	50gm
C Tutti Frutti	487		2	2	2	2	2	2	x	50gm
D Jelly Baby	496		1	1	1	1	1	1	x	50gm
E Midget Gem	497		1	1	1	2	2	2	x	50gm

NEEDLES
1 pair 2¼mm (no 13) (US 1) needles
1 pair 2¾mm (no 12) (US 2) needles

TENSION
30 sts and 38 rows to 10 cm measured over st st using 2¾mm (US 2) needles.

BACK
Using 2¼mm (US 1) needles and yarn A cast on
126 [130: 138: 146: 154: 162] sts.
Row 1 (RS): K2, ★P2, K2, rep from ★ to end.
Row 2: P2, ★K2, P2, rep from ★ to end.
These 2 rows form rib.
Cont in rib for a further 4 rows, dec 1 st at each end of 3rd of these rows
and ending with RS facing for next row.
124 [128: 136: 144: 152: 160] sts.
Knit one row, dec [inc: dec: dec: inc: inc] 1 st at centre of row and ending
with **WS** facing for next row. 123 [129: 135: 143: 153: 161] sts.
Change to 2¾mm (US 2) needles.
Noting that chart row 1 is a **WS** row, beg and ending rows as indicated, using
a combination of the **fairisle** (for rows 17 to 28) and the **intarsia** (for rows
47 to 66) techniques as described on the information page and repeating the
66 row patt repeat throughout, now work in patt from chart as folls:
Dec 1 st at each end of 2nd and 3 foll 4th rows.
115 [121: 127: 135: 145: 153] sts.
Work 9 rows, ending with RS facing for next row.
Inc 1 st at each end of next and every foll 10th row until there are
127 [133: 139: 147: 157: 165] sts, taking inc sts into patt.
Cont straight until back meas 26 [26: 25: 28: 27: 29] cm, ending with RS
facing for next row.
Shape armholes
Keeping patt correct, cast off 5 [6: 6: 7: 7: 8] sts at beg of next 2 rows.
117 [121: 127: 133: 143: 149] sts.★★
Dec 1 st at each end of next 7 [7: 9: 9: 11: 11] rows, then on foll 5 [5: 5:
6: 6: 7] alt rows. 93 [97: 99: 103: 109: 113] sts.
Cont straight until armhole meas 18 [18: 19: 19: 20: 20] cm, ending with
RS facing for next row.
Shape shoulders and back neck
Next row (RS): Cast off 6 [7: 7: 8: 9: 9] sts, patt until there are 16 [17:
18: 19: 20: 22] sts on right needle and turn, leaving rem sts on a holder.
Work each side of neck separately.
Dec 1 st at neck edge of next 3 rows **and at same time** cast off 6 [7: 7:
8: 9: 9] sts at beg of 2nd row.
Cast off rem 7 [7: 8: 8: 8: 10] sts.
With RS facing, rejoin appropriate yarn(s) to rem sts, cast off centre

49 [49: 49: 49: 51: 51] sts, patt to end.
Complete to match first side, reversing shapings.

FRONT
Work as given for back to ★★.
Dec 1 st at each end of next 7 [7: 8: 8: 8: 8] rows.
103 [107: 111: 117: 127: 133] sts.
Work 1 [1: 0: 0: 0: 0] row, ending with RS facing for next row.
Shape neck
Next row (RS): Work 2 tog, patt 39 [41: 43: 46: 50: 53] sts and turn,
leaving rem sts on a holder.
Work each side of neck separately.
Keeping patt correct, dec 1 st at neck edge of next 8 rows, then on foll
6 alt rows, then on 3 foll 4th rows **and at same time** dec 1 st at armhole
edge of 2nd [2nd: 2nd: 2nd: next: next] and foll 0 [0: 0: 0: 1: 1] row, then
on foll 3 [3: 4: 5: 6: 7] alt rows. 19 [21: 22: 24: 26: 28] sts.
Cont straight until front matches back to beg of shoulder shaping, ending
with RS facing for next row.
Shape shoulder
Cast off 6 [7: 7: 8: 9: 9] sts at beg of next and foll alt row.
Work 1 row.
Cast off rem 7 [7: 8: 8: 8: 10] sts.
With RS facing, rejoin appropriate yarn(s) to rem sts, cast off centre
21 [21: 21: 21: 23: 23] sts, patt to last 2 sts, work 2 tog.
Complete to match first side, reversing shapings.

SLEEVES
Using 2¼mm (US 1) needles and yarn A cast on 62 [62: 66: 66: 70: 70] sts.
Work in rib as given for back, shaping sides by inc 1 st at each end of
9th and 9 foll 6th rows, taking inc sts into rib.
82 [82: 86: 86: 90: 90] sts.
Work 5 rows, ending with RS facing for next row.
Break off yarn A and join in yarn B.
Change to 2¾mm (US 2) needles.
Beg with a K row, work in st st, shaping sides by inc 1 st at each end of
3rd and every foll 6th row to 92 [100: 100: 108: 108: 116] sts, then on every
foll 8th row until there are 106 [108: 112: 114: 118: 120] sts.
Cont straight until sleeve meas 45 [45: 46: 46: 47: 47] cm, ending with RS

facing for next row.

Shape top

Cast off 5 [6: 6: 7: 7: 8] sts at beg of next 2 rows.
96 [96: 100: 100: 104: 104] sts.
Dec 1 st at each end of next 5 rows, then on every foll alt row until 70 sts
rem, then on foll 17 rows, ending with RS facing for next row. 36 sts.
Cast off 5 sts at beg of next 4 rows.
Cast off rem 16 sts.

MAKING UP
Press as described on the information page.
Join right shoulder seam using back stitch, or mattress stitch if preferred.

Neckband

With RS facing, using 2¼mm (US 1) needles and yarn A, pick up and knit
51 [51: 53: 55: 57: 57] sts down left side of neck, 21 [21: 21: 21: 23: 23] sts
from front, 51 [51: 53: 55: 57: 57] sts up right side of neck, then 55 [55: 55:
55: 57: 57] sts from back. 178 [178: 182: 186: 194: 194] sts.
Beg with row 2, work in rib as given for back for 5 rows, ending with RS
facing for next row.
Cast off in rib.
See information page for finishing instructions, setting in sleeves using the
set-in method.

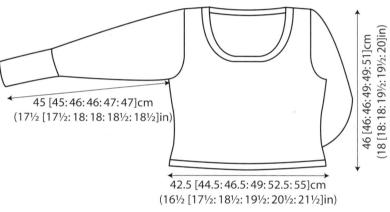

45 [45: 46: 46: 47: 47]cm
(17½ [17½: 18: 18: 18½: 18½]in)

46 [46: 46: 49: 49: 51]cm
(18 [18: 18: 19½: 19½: 20]in)

42.5 [44.5: 46.5: 49: 52.5: 55]cm
(16½ [17½: 18½: 19½: 20½: 21½]in)

key

row 1 - 15 (using yarn B)
☐ K on RS, P on WS
⊡ P on RS

rows 16 - 29
☐ C ⎤
⊠ D ⎬ all K on RS, P on WS
◉ E ⎦

rows 30 - 46 (using yarn E)
☐ K on RS, P on WS
⊘ P2tog
⊠ P2tog tbl
◉ yrn
△ sl 1, P2tog, psso

rows 47 - 66
☐ A ⎤
⊠ C ⎪
⊡ B ⎬ all K on RS, P on WS
◉ D ⎦

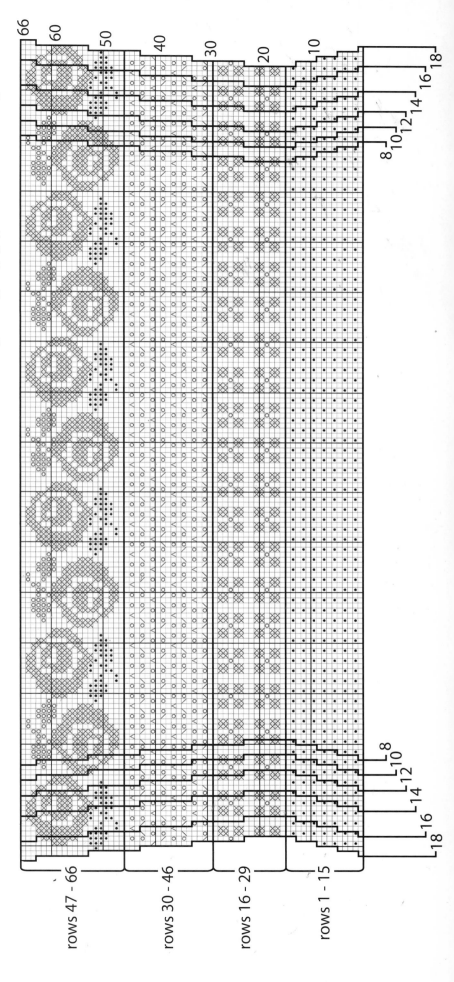

YARN

	S	M	L	XL	XXL	
To fit bust	81-86	91-97	102-107	112-117	122-127	cm
	32-34	36-38	40-42	44-46	48-50	in
Rowan Fine Milk Cotton						
	11	12	13	14	15	x 50gm

(photographed in Snow 493)

NEEDLES

1 pair 2¼mm (no 13) (US 1) needles
1 pair 2¾mm (no 12) (US 2) needles
2.50mm (no 12) (US C2) crochet hook

TENSION

30 sts and 38 rows to 10 cm measured over st st using 2¾mm (US 2) needles

UK CROCHET ABBREVIATIONS

ch = chain

BACK

Using 2¼mm (US 1) needles cast on 132 [148: 166: 184: 204] sts.
Work in g st for 6 rows, ending with RS facing for next row.
Change to 2¾mm (US 2) needles.
Row 7 (RS): K6 [2: 11: 8: 6], (K1 [2: 2: 2: 2], M1, K3 [3: 3: 3: 4], M1, K1 [1: 1: 2: 2]) 24 times, K6 [2: 11: 8: 6].
180 [196: 214: 232: 252] sts.
Beg with a P row, cont in st st until back meas 10 cm, ending with RS facing for next row.
Dec 1 st at each end of next and every foll 6th row until 156 [172: 190: 208: 228] sts rem.
Cont straight until back meas 32 [33: 34: 35: 36] cm, ending with RS facing for next row.
Shape armholes
Cast off 10 [11: 12: 13: 14] sts at beg of next 2 rows.
136 [150: 166: 182: 200] sts.★★
Dec 1 st at each end of next 9 [11: 13: 15: 17] rows, then on foll 0 [2: 3: 5: 7] alt rows. 118 [124: 134: 142: 152] sts.
Work 5 rows, ending with RS facing for next row.
Inc 1 st at each end of next and 9 foll 4th rows.
138 [144: 154: 162: 172] sts.
Cont straight until armhole meas 18 [19: 20: 21: 22] cm, ending with **WS** facing for next row.
Next row (WS): P28 [31: 36: 40: 45], (P2tog, P1) 13 times, (P2tog) twice, (P1, P2tog) 13 times, P to end.
110 [116: 126: 134: 144] sts.
Shape back neck
Next row (RS): K27 [30: 34: 38: 42] and turn, leaving rem sts on a holder.
Work each side of neck separately.
Next row: P3tog, P to end.
Next row: K to last 2 sts, K2tog. 24 [27: 31: 35: 39] sts.
Rep last 2 rows twice more, and then first of these 2 rows again, ending with RS facing for next row. 16 [19: 23: 27: 31] sts.

Shape shoulder
Cast off 5 [6: 7: 9: 10] sts at beg of next and foll alt row **and at same time** dec 1 st at neck edge of first of these rows.
Work 1 row.

Cast off rem 5 [6: 8: 8: 10] sts.
With RS facing, rejoin yarn to rem sts, cast off centre 56 [56: 58: 58: 60] sts, K to end.
Complete to match first side, reversing shapings.

FRONT

Work as given for back to ★★.
Dec 1 st at each end of next 9 [11: 13: 15: 17] rows, then on foll 8 [10: 11: 13: 15] alt rows. 102 [108: 118: 126: 136] sts.
Cont straight until 30 rows less have been worked than on back to beg of shoulder shaping, ending with RS facing for next row.
Shape neck
Next row (RS): K38 [41: 45: 49: 53] and turn, leaving rem sts on a holder.
Work each side of neck separately.
Dec 2 sts (by working 3 sts tog) at neck edge of next 5 rows, then dec 1 st at neck edge of foll 7 rows, then on foll 4 alt rows, then on 2 foll 4th rows. 15 [18: 22: 26: 30] sts.
Work 1 row, ending with RS facing for next row.
Shape shoulder
Cast off 1 [1: 2: 2: 2] sts at beg of next and foll 6 [3: 9: 6: 2] alt rows, then 2 [2: 0: 3: 3] sts at beg of foll 3 [6: 0: 3: 7] alt rows.
Work 1 row.
Cast off rem 2 [2: 2: 3: 3] sts.
With RS facing, rejoin yarn to rem sts, cast off centre 26 [26: 28: 28: 30] sts, K to end.
Complete to match first side, reversing shapings.

SLEEVES

Using 2¼mm (US 1) needles cast on 60 [62: 64: 66: 68] sts.
Work in g st for 6 rows, ending with RS facing for next row.
Change to 2¾mm (US 2) needles.
Row 7 (RS): Inc once in each st to end.
120 [124: 128: 132: 136] sts.
Beg with a P row, cont in st st until sleeve meas 49 [50: 51: 51: 51] cm, ending with RS facing for next row.
Shape top
Cast off 10 [11: 12: 13: 14] sts at beg of next 2 rows.
100 [102: 104: 106: 108] sts.

Dec 1 st at each end of next 3 rows, then on every foll alt row until 90 sts rem, then on foll 5 rows, ending with RS facing for next row. 80 sts.
Cast off 3 sts at beg of next 2 rows, then 4 sts at beg of foll 2 rows, then 5 sts at beg of foll 8 rows.
Cast off rem 26 sts.

MAKING UP
Press as described on the information page.
Join right shoulder seam using back stitch, or mattress stitch if preferred.
Neckband
With RS facing and using 2¼mm (US 1) needles, pick up and knit 45 sts down left side of neck, 26 [26: 28: 28: 30] sts from front, 45 sts up right side of neck, then 72 [72: 74: 74: 76] sts from back.

188 [188: 192: 192: 196] sts.
Row 1 (WS): K72 [72: 74: 74: 76], (K2tog, K1) 15 times, K26 [26: 28: 28: 30], (K1, K2tog) 15 times. 158 [158: 162: 162: 166] sts.
Work in g st for a further 3 rows, ending with **WS** facing for next row.
Cast off knitwise (on **WS**).
See information page for finishing instructions, setting in sleeves using the set-in method.
Tie (optional)
Using 2.50mm (US C2) crochet hook, make a ch approx 160 [170: 180: 190: 200] cm long.
Fasten off.
Beg 20 cm in from right side seam, thread tie in and out of knitting (by gently easing sts apart) just above g st hem border as in photograph.

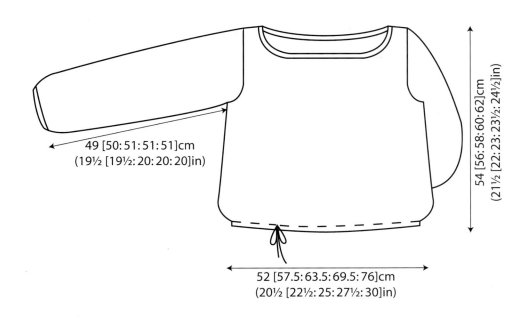

49 [50: 51: 51: 51]cm
(19½ [19½: 20: 20: 20]in)

54 [56: 58: 60: 62]cm
(21½ [22: 23: 23½: 24½]in)

52 [57.5: 63.5: 69.5: 76]cm
(20½ [22½: 25: 27½: 30]in)

YARN

	8	10	12	14	16	18	20	22	
To fit bust	81	86	91	97	102	107	112	117	cm
	32	34	36	38	40	42	44	46	in

Rowan Fine Milk Cotton

Jumper	9	9	10	10	11	12	12	13 x 50gm
(photographed in Humbugs 484)

Cardigan	11	11	11	12	12	13	14	15 x 50gm
(photographed in Shrimps 483)

NEEDLES

1 pair 2¼mm (no 13) (US 1) needles, 1 pair 2¾mm (no 12) (US 2) needles
Jumper only: 2¼mm (no 13) (US 1) circular needle

BUTTONS – cardigan only: 4 x BN1152

TENSION

35 sts and 40 rows to 10 cm measured over patt using 2¾mm (US 2) needles.

SPECIAL ABBREVIATIONS

bind 3 – slip 1 st purlwise with yarn at back (WS) of work, K1, yfwd, K1, lift slipped st over the (K1, yfwd, K1) and off right needle.

Jumper

BACK

Using 2¼mm (US 1) needles cast on 129 [132: 139: 148: 156: 165: 175: 184] sts.
Work in g st for 9 rows, ending with **WS** facing for next row.
Change to 2¾mm (US 2) needles.
Next row (WS): P4 [3: 3: 5: 3: 4: 3: 5], M1, (P6, M1) 20 [21: 22: 23: 25: 26: 28: 29] times, P5 [3: 4: 5: 3: 5: 4: 5].
150 [154: 162: 172: 182: 192: 204: 214] sts.
Cont in patt as folls:
Row 1 (RS): P1 [3: 2: 2: 2: 2: 3: 3], K3, ★P2, K3, rep from ★ to last
1 [3: 2: 2: 2: 2: 3: 3] sts, P1 [3: 2: 2: 2: 2: 3: 3].
Row 2: K1 [3: 2: 2: 2: 2: 3: 3], P3, ★K2, P3, rep from ★ to last 1 [3: 2: 2: 2: 2: 3: 3] sts, K1 [3: 2: 2: 2: 2: 3: 3].
Row 3: P1 [3: 2: 2: 2: 2: 3: 3], bind 3, ★P2, bind 3, rep from ★ to last
1 [3: 2: 2: 2: 2: 3: 3] sts, P1 [3: 2: 2: 2: 2: 3: 3].
Row 4: As row 2.
These 4 rows form patt.
Cont in patt, shaping side seams by dec 1 st at each end of 3rd and every foll 4th row until 136 [140: 148: 158: 168: 178: 190: 200] sts rem.
Work 11 rows, ending with RS facing for next row.
Inc 1 st at each end of next and every foll 8th row until there are 150 [154: 162: 172: 182: 192: 204: 214] sts, taking inc sts into patt.
Cont straight until back meas 29 [29: 28: 31: 30: 32: 31: 33] cm, ending with RS facing for next row.

Shape armholes

Keeping patt correct, cast off 7 [8: 8: 9: 9: 10: 10: 11] sts at beg of next
2 rows. 136 [138: 146: 154: 164: 172: 184: 192] sts.
Dec 1 st at each end of next 7 [7: 9: 9: 11: 11: 13: 13] rows, then on foll
7 [6: 6: 8: 8: 9: 11: 12] alt rows.
108 [112: 116: 120: 126: 132: 136: 142] sts.★★
Cont straight until armhole meas 17 [17: 18: 18: 19: 19: 20: 20] cm, ending with RS facing for next row.

Shape back neck

Next row (RS): Patt 24 [26: 28: 30: 30: 33: 35: 38] sts and turn, leaving rem sts on a holder.
Work each side of neck separately.
Work 9 rows, ending with RS facing for next row.

Shape shoulder

Cast off 8 [9: 9: 10: 10: 11: 12: 13] sts at beg of next and foll alt row.

Work 1 row.
Cast off rem 8 [8: 10: 10: 10: 11: 11: 12] sts.
With RS facing, rejoin yarn to rem sts, cast off centre 60 [60: 60: 60: 66: 66: 66: 66] sts, patt to end.
Complete to match first side, reversing shapings.

FRONT

Work as given for back to ★★.
Work 5 [7: 9: 5: 7: 5: 3: 1] rows, ending with RS facing for next row.

Shape neck

Next row (RS): Patt 24 [26: 28: 30: 30: 33: 35: 38] sts and turn, leaving rem sts on a holder.
Work each side of neck separately.
Cont straight until front matches back to beg of shoulder shaping, ending with RS facing for next row.

Shape shoulder

Cast off 8 [9: 9: 10: 10: 11: 12: 13] sts at beg of next and foll alt row.
Work 1 row.
Cast off rem 8 [8: 10: 10: 10: 11: 11: 12] sts.
With RS facing, rejoin yarn to rem sts, cast off centre 60 [60: 60: 60: 66: 66: 66: 66] sts, patt to end.
Complete to match first side, reversing shapings.

SLEEVES

Using 2¼mm (US 1) needles cast on 103 [103: 107: 108: 110: 112: 117: 119] sts.
Work in g st for 9 rows, ending with **WS** facing for next row.
Change to 2¾mm (US 2) needles.
Next row (WS): P3 [3: 5: 3: 4: 5: 4: 5], M1, (P6, M1) 16 [16: 16: 17: 17: 17: 18: 18] times, P4 [4: 6: 3: 4: 5: 5: 6].
120 [120: 124: 126: 128: 130: 136: 138] sts.
Cont in patt as folls:
Row 1 (RS): P1 [1: 0: 0: 0: 1: 0: 0], K3 [3: 1: 2: 3: 3: 2: 3], ★P2, K3, rep from ★ to last 1 [1: 3: 4: 0: 1: 4: 0] sts, P1 [1: 2: 2: 0: 1: 2: 0], K0 [0: 1: 2: 0: 0: 2: 0].
Row 2: K1 [1: 0: 0: 0: 1: 0: 0], P3 [3: 1: 2: 3: 3: 2: 3], ★K2, P3, rep from ★ to last 1 [1: 3: 4: 0: 1: 4: 0] sts, K1 [1: 2: 2: 0: 1: 2: 0], P0 [0: 1: 2: 0: 0: 2: 0].
Row 3: P1 [1: 0: 0: 0: 1: 0: 0], (bind 3) 1 [1: 0: 0: 1: 1: 0: 1] times, K0 [0: 1: 2: 0: 0: 2: 0], ★P2, bind 3, rep from ★ to last 1 [1: 3: 4: 0: 1: 4: 0] sts, P1 [1: 2: 2: 0: 1: 2: 0], K0 [0: 1: 2: 0: 0: 2: 0].
Row 4: As row 2.

These 4 rows form patt.

Cont in patt, shaping sides by inc 1 st at each end of 3rd [3rd: 3rd: 7th: next: next: 7th: 7th] and every foll 12th [10th: 10th: 10th: 10th: 10th: 10th: 10th] row to 132 [134: 134: 140: 144: 146: 150: 152] sts, then on every foll – [-: 12th: –: –: –: –: –] row until there are – [-: 138: –: –: –: –: –] sts, taking inc sts into patt.

Cont straight until sleeve meas 24 [24: 25: 25: 26: 26: 25: 25] cm, ending with RS facing for next row.

Shape top

Keeping patt correct, cast off 7 [8: 8: 9: 9: 10: 10: 11] sts at beg of next 2 rows. 118 [118: 122: 122: 126: 126: 130: 130] sts.

Dec 1 st at each end of next 7 rows, then on every foll alt row until 94 sts rem, then on foll 25 rows, ending with RS facing for next row. 44 sts.

Cast off 6 sts at beg of next 4 rows.

Cast off rem 20 sts.

MAKING UP

Press as described on the information page.

Join both shoulder seams using back stitch, or mattress stitch if preferred.

Neckband

With RS facing and using 2¼mm (US 1) circular needle, beg and ending at left shoulder seam, pick up and knit 42 sts down left side of front neck placing marker on last of these sts, 52 [52: 52: 52: 57: 57: 57: 57] sts from front, 42 sts up right side of front neck placing marker on first of these sts, 12 sts down right side of back neck placing marker on last of these sts, 52 [52: 52: 52: 57: 57: 57: 57] sts from back, then 12 sts up left side of back neck placing marker on first of these sts. 212 [212: 212: 212: 222: 222: 222: 222] sts.

Round 1 (RS): (K to within 2 sts of marked st, sl 1, K1, psso, K marked st, K2tog) 4 times, K to end.

Round 2: (P to marked st, K marked st) 4 times, P to end.

Rep last 2 rounds 3 times more, then round 1 again.

172 [172: 172: 172: 182: 182: 182: 182] sts.

Cast off purlwise (on RS).

See information page for finishing instructions, setting in sleeves using the set–in method.

Cardigan

BACK

Using 2¼mm (US 1) needles cast on 132 [136: 143: 151: 160: 168: 179: 187] sts.

Work in g st for 9 rows, ending with **WS** facing for next row.

Change to 2¾mm (US 2) needles.

Next row (WS): P3 [5: 5: 3: 5: 3: 5: 3], M1, (P6, M1) 21 [21: 22: 24: 25: 27: 28: 30] times, P3 [5: 6: 4: 5: 3: 6: 4].

154 [158: 166: 176: 186: 196: 208: 218] sts.

Cont in patt as folls:

Row 1 (RS): P3 [5: 4: 4: 4: 4: 5: 5], K3, ★P2, K3, rep from ★ to last 3 [5: 4: 4: 4: 4: 5: 5] sts, P3 [5: 4: 4: 4: 4: 5: 5].

Row 2: K3 [5: 4: 4: 4: 4: 5: 5], P3, ★K2, P3, rep from ★ to last 3 [5: 4: 4: 4: 4: 5: 5] sts, K3 [5: 4: 4: 4: 4: 5: 5].

Row 3: P3 [5: 4: 4: 4: 4: 5: 5], bind 3, ★P2, bind 3, rep from ★ to last 3 [5: 4: 4: 4: 4: 5: 5] sts, P3 [5: 4: 4: 4: 4: 5: 5].

Row 4: As row 2.

These 4 rows form patt.

Cont in patt, shaping side seams by dec 1 st at each end of 3rd and every foll 4th row until 140 [144: 152: 162: 172: 182: 194: 204] sts rem.

Work 11 rows, ending with RS facing for next row.

Inc 1 st at each end of next and every foll 8th row until there are 154 [158: 166: 176: 186: 196: 208: 218] sts, taking inc sts into patt.

Cont straight until back meas 31 [31: 30: 33: 32: 34: 33: 35] cm, ending with RS facing for next row.

Shape armholes

Keeping patt correct, cast off 7 [8: 8: 9: 9: 10: 10: 11] sts at beg of next 2 rows. 140 [142: 150: 158: 168: 176: 188: 196] sts.

Dec 1 st at each end of next 9 [9: 11: 11: 13: 13: 15: 15] rows, then on foll 7 [6: 6: 8: 8: 9: 11: 12] alt rows.

108 [112: 116: 120: 126: 132: 136: 142] sts.

Cont straight until armhole meas 17 [17: 18: 18: 19: 19: 20: 20] cm, ending with RS facing for next row.

Shape back neck

Next row (RS): Patt 24 [26: 28: 30: 30: 33: 35: 38] sts and turn, leaving rem sts on a holder.

Work each side of neck separately.

Work 9 rows, ending with RS facing for next row.

Shape shoulder

Cast off 8 [9: 9: 10: 10: 11: 12: 13] sts at beg of next and foll alt row.

Work 1 row.

Cast off rem 8 [8: 10: 10: 10: 11: 11: 12] sts.

With RS facing, rejoin yarn to rem sts, cast off centre 60 [60: 60: 60: 66: 66: 66: 66] sts, patt to end.

Complete to match first side, reversing shapings.

LEFT FRONT

Using 2¼mm (US 1) needles cast on 66 [68: 72: 76: 80: 84: 90: 94] sts.

Work in g st for 9 rows, ending with **WS** facing for next row.

Change to 2¾mm (US 2) needles.

Next row (WS): P3 [4: 6: 5: 4: 3: 6: 5], M1, (P6, M1) 10 [10: 10: 11: 12: 13: 13: 14] times, P3 [4: 6: 5: 4: 3: 6: 5].

77 [79: 83: 88: 93: 98: 104: 109] sts.

Cont in patt as folls:

Row 1 (RS): P3 [5: 4: 4: 4: 4: 5: 5], K3, ★P2, K3, rep from ★ to last st, P1.

Row 2: K1, P3, ★K2, P3, rep from ★ to last 3 [5: 4: 4: 4: 4: 5: 5] sts, K3 [5: 4: 4: 4: 4: 5: 5].

Row 3: P3 [5: 4: 4: 4: 4: 5: 5], bind 3, ★P2, bind 3, rep from ★ to last st, P1.

Row 4: As row 2.

These 4 rows form patt.

Cont in patt, shaping side seam by dec 1 st at beg of 3rd and every foll 4th row until 70 [72: 76: 81: 86: 91: 97: 102] sts rem.

Work 11 rows, ending with RS facing for next row.

Inc 1 st at beg of next and every foll 8th row until there are 77 [79: 83: 88: 93: 98: 104: 109] sts, taking inc sts into patt.

Cont straight until left front matches back to beg of armhole shaping, ending with RS facing for next row.

Shape armhole

Keeping patt correct, cast off 7 [8: 8: 9: 9: 10: 10: 11] sts at beg of next row. 70 [71: 75: 79: 84: 88: 94: 98] sts.

Work 1 row.

Dec 1 st at armhole edge of next 9 [9: 11: 11: 13: 13: 15: 15] rows, then on foll 7 [6: 6: 8: 8: 9: 11: 12] alt rows. 54 [56: 58: 60: 63: 66: 68: 71] sts.

Work 4 [6: 8: 4: 6: 4: 2: 0] rows, ending with **WS** facing for next row.

Shape neck

Keeping patt correct, cast off 30 [30: 30: 30: 33: 33: 33: 33] sts at beg of next row. 24 [26: 28: 30: 30: 33: 35: 38] sts.

Cont straight until left front matches back to beg of shoulder shaping, ending with RS facing for next row.

Shape shoulder

Cast off 8 [9: 9: 10: 10: 11: 12: 13] sts at beg of next and foll alt row.

Work 1 row.

Cast off rem 8 [8: 10: 10: 10: 11: 11: 12] sts.

RIGHT FRONT

Using 2¼mm (US 1) needles cast on 66 [68: 72: 76: 80: 84: 90: 94] sts.

Work in g st for 9 rows, ending with **WS** facing for next row.
Change to 2¾mm (US 2) needles.
Next row (WS): P3 [4: 6: 5: 4: 3: 6: 5], M1, (P6, M1) 10 [10: 10: 11: 12: 13: 13: 14] times, P3 [4: 6: 5: 4: 3: 6: 5].
77 [79: 83: 88: 93: 98: 104: 109] sts.
Cont in patt as folls:
Row 1 (RS): P1, K3, ★P2, K3, rep from ★ to last 3 [5: 4: 4: 4: 4: 5: 5] sts, P3 [5: 4: 4: 4: 4: 5: 5].
Row 2: K3 [5: 4: 4: 4: 4: 5: 5], P3, ★K2, P3, rep from ★ to last st, K1.
Row 3: P1, bind 3, ★P2, bind 3, rep from ★ to last 3 [5: 4: 4: 4: 4: 5: 5] sts, P3 [5: 4: 4: 4: 4: 5: 5].
Row 4: As row 2.
These 4 rows form patt.
Cont in patt, shaping side seam by dec 1 st at end of 3rd and every foll 4th row until 70 [72: 76: 81: 86: 91: 97: 102] sts rem.
Complete to match left front, reversing shapings.

SLEEVES
Using 2¼mm (US 1) needles cast on 84 [84: 88: 88: 91: 91: 95: 95] sts.
Work in g st for 9 rows, ending with **WS** facing for next row.
Change to 2¾mm (US 2) needles.
Next row (WS): P3 [3: 5: 5: 3: 3: 5: 5], M1, (P6, M1) 13 [13: 13: 13: 14: 14: 14: 14] times, P3 [3: 5: 5: 4: 4: 6: 6].
98 [98: 102: 102: 106: 106: 110: 110] sts.
Cont in patt as folls:
Row 1 (RS): P0 [0: 0: 0: 0: 0: 1: 1], K3 [3: 0: 0: 2: 2: 3: 3], ★P2, K3, rep from ★ to last 0 [0: 2: 2: 4: 4: 1: 1] sts, P0 [0: 2: 2: 2: 2: 1: 1], K0 [0: 0: 0: 2: 2: 0: 0].
Row 2: K0 [0: 0: 0: 0: 0: 1: 1], P3 [3: 0: 0: 2: 2: 3: 3], ★K2, P3, rep from ★ to last 0 [0: 2: 2: 4: 4: 1: 1] sts, K0 [0: 2: 2: 2: 2: 1: 1], P0 [0: 0: 0: 2: 2: 0: 0].
Row 3: P0 [0: 0: 0: 0: 0: 1: 1], K0 [0: 0: 0: 2: 2: 0: 0], (bind 3) 1 [1: 0: 0: 0: 0: 1: 1] times, ★P2, bind 3, rep from ★ to last 0 [0: 2: 2: 4: 4: 1: 1] sts, P0 [0: 2: 2: 2: 2: 1: 1], K0 [0: 0: 0: 2: 2: 0: 0].
Row 4: As row 2.
These 4 rows form patt.
Cont in patt, shaping sides by inc 1 st at each end of 3rd [3rd: 3rd: 3rd: 3rd: 3rd: 3rd: next] and every foll 8th [8th: 8th: 8th: 8th: 8th: 8th: 6th] row to 112 [122: 122: 132: 132: 142: 150: 118] sts, then on every foll 10th [10th: 10th: 10th: 10th: 10th: -: 8th] row until there are 132 [134: 138: 140: 144: 146: -: 152] sts, taking inc sts into patt.
Cont straight until sleeve meas 46 [46: 47: 47: 48: 48: 47: 47] cm, ending with RS facing for next row.
Shape top
Keeping patt correct, cast off 7 [8: 8: 9: 9: 10: 10: 11] sts at beg of next 2 rows. 118 [118: 122: 122: 126: 126: 130: 130] sts.
Dec 1 st at each end of next 14 [14: 16: 16: 18: 18: 20: 20] rows, ending

with RS facing for next row. 90 sts.
Cast off 6 sts at beg of next 8 rows.
Cast off rem 42 sts.

MAKING UP
Press as described on the information page.
Join both shoulder seams using back stitch, or mattress stitch if preferred.
Neckband
With RS facing and using 2¼mm (US 1) needles, beg and ending at front opening edges, pick up and knit 26 [26: 26: 26: 29: 29: 29: 29] sts from right front, 42 sts up right side of front neck placing marker on first of these sts, 12 sts down right side of back neck placing marker on last of these sts, 52 [52: 52: 52: 57: 57: 57: 57] sts from back, 12 sts up left side of back neck placing marker on first of these sts, 42 sts down left side of front neck placing marker on last of these sts, then 26 [26: 26: 26: 29: 29: 29: 29] sts from right front.
212 [212: 212: 212: 223: 223: 223: 223] sts.
Row 1 (WS): (K to marked st, P marked st) 4 times, K to end.
Row 2: (K to within 2 sts of marked st, sl 1, K1, psso, K marked st, K2tog) 4 times, K to end.
Rep last 2 rows 3 times more. 180 [180: 180: 180: 191: 191: 191: 191] sts.
Cast off knitwise (on **WS**).
Button band
With RS facing and using 2¼mm (US 1) needles, pick up and knit 118 [118: 118: 127: 127: 133: 133: 139] sts evenly down left front opening edge, from top of neckband to cast-on edge.
Work in g st for 8 rows, ending with **WS** facing for next row.
Cast off knitwise (on **WS**).
Buttonhole band
With RS facing and using 2¼mm (US 1) needles, pick up and knit 118 [118: 118: 127: 127: 133: 133: 139] sts evenly up right front opening edge, from cast-on edge to top of neckband.
Work in g st for 3 rows, ending with RS facing for next row.
Row 4 (RS): K to last 59 sts, cast off 2 sts (to make first buttonhole – cast on 2 sts over these cast-off sts on next row), K until there are 8 sts on right needle after cast-off, cast off 2 sts (to make 2nd buttonhole – cast on 2 sts over these cast-off sts on next row), K until there are 33 sts on right needle after cast-off, cast off 2 sts (to make 3rd buttonhole – cast on 2 sts over these cast-off sts on next row), K until there are 8 sts on right needle after cast-off, cast off 2 sts (to make 4th buttonhole – cast on 2 sts over these cast-off sts on next row), K to end.
Work in g st for a further 4 rows, ending with **WS** facing for next row.
Cast off knitwise (on **WS**).
See information page for finishing instructions, setting in sleeves using the set-in method.

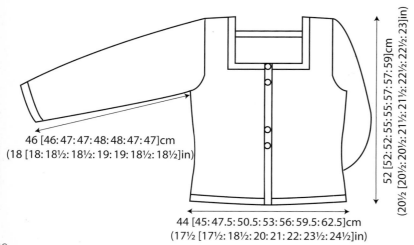

46 [46: 47: 47: 48: 48: 47: 47]cm
(18 [18: 18½: 18½: 19: 19: 18½: 18½]in)

52 [52: 52: 55: 55: 57: 57: 59]cm
(20½ [20½: 20½: 21½: 21½: 22½: 22½: 23]in)

44 [45: 47.5: 50.5: 53: 56: 59.5: 62.5]cm
(17½ [17½: 18½: 20: 21: 22: 23½: 24½]in)

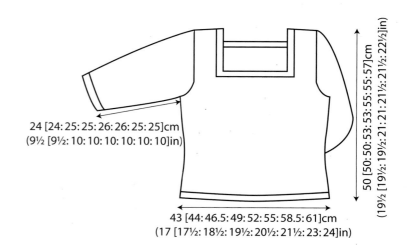

24 [24: 25: 25: 26: 26: 25: 25]cm
(9½ [9½: 10: 10: 10: 10: 10: 10]in)

50 [50: 50: 53: 53: 55: 55: 57]cm
(19½ [19½: 19½: 21: 21: 21½: 21½: 22½]in)

43 [44: 46.5: 49: 52: 55: 58.5: 61]cm
(17 [17½: 18½: 19½: 20½: 21½: 23: 24]in)

YARN

Caitlyn

To fit bust	8	10	12	14	16	18	
	81	86	91	97	102	107	cm
	32	34	36	38	40	42	in

Rowan Fine Milk Cotton

			8	10	12	14	16	18		
A	Jelly Baby	496	5	5	5	5	5	6	x	50gm
B	Water Bomb	498	2	2	2	2	2	2	x	50gm
C	Tutti Frutti	487	2	2	2	2	2	2	x	50gm
D	Midget Gem	497	1	1	1	1	1	1	x	50gm
E	Snow	493	1	1	1	1	1	1	x	50gm

NEEDLES - 1 pair 2¼mm (no 13) (US 1) needles, 1 pair 2¾mm (no 12) (US 2) needles & 2.50mm (no 12) (US C2) crochet hook

BUTTONS – 2 x BN1028

TENSION - 30 sts and 38 rows to 10 cm measured over st st using 2 ¾mm (US 2) needles.

UK CROCHET ABBREVIATIONS

ch = chain; **dc** = double crochet; **ss** = slip stitch; **tr** = treble.

Caitlyn

BACK

Using 2¼mm (US 1) needles and yarn B cast on 127 [133: 139: 147: 157: 165] sts.

Row 1 (RS): K0 [0: 0: 1: 0: 1], *P1, K2, rep from * to last 1 [1: 1: 2: 1: 2] sts, P1, K0 [0: 0: 1: 0: 1].

Row 2: P0 [0: 0: 1: 0: 1], *K1, P2, rep from * to last 1 [1: 1: 2: 1: 2] sts, K1, P0 [0: 0: 1: 0: 1].

These 2 rows form rib.

Keeping rib correct and joining in and breaking off colours as required, work in stripes as folls:

Using yarn E, work 1 row.
Using yarn B, work 3 rows.
Using yarn E, work 2 rows.
Using yarn B, work 7 rows, ending with **WS** facing for next row.
Break off yarns B and E and join in yarn A.

Row 16 (WS): Purl.

Change to 2¾mm (US 2) needles.

Now work in patt as folls:

Row 1 (RS): K0 [2: 0: 0: 2: 0], P2 [3: 2: 0: 3: 3], *K3, P3, rep from * to last 5 [2: 5: 3: 2: 0] sts, K3 [2: 3: 3: 2: 0], P2 [0: 2: 0: 0: 0].

Row 2: P0 [2: 0: 0: 2: 0], K2 [3: 2: 0: 3: 3], *P3, K3, rep from * to last 5 [2: 5: 3: 2: 0] sts, P3 [2: 3: 3: 2: 0], K2 [0: 2: 0: 0: 0].

Rows 3 and 4: As row 1.
Row 5: As row 2.
Row 6: As row 1.

These 6 rows form patt.

Work in patt for a further 9 rows, ending after patt row 3 and with **WS** facing for next row.

Beg with a P row, work in st st until back meas 28 [28: 27: 30: 29: 31] cm, ending with RS facing for next row.

Shape armholes

Cast off 5 [6: 6: 7: 7: 8] sts at beg of next 2 rows.

117 [121: 127: 133: 143: 149] sts.★★

Dec 1 st at each end of next 7 [7: 9: 9: 11: 11] rows, then on foll 5 [5: 5: 6: 6: 7] alt rows. 93 [97: 99: 103: 109: 113] sts.

Cont straight until armhole meas 18 [18: 19: 19: 20: 20] cm, ending with RS facing for next row.

Shape shoulders and back neck

Cast off 6 [7: 7: 8: 9: 9] sts at beg of next 2 rows.

81 [83: 85: 87: 91: 95] sts.

Next row (RS): Cast off 6 [7: 7: 8: 9: 9] sts, K until there are 11 [11: 12: 12: 12: 14] sts on right needle and turn, leaving rem sts on a holder.

Work each side of neck separately.

Cast off 4 sts at beg of next row.

Cast off rem 7 [7: 8: 8: 8: 10] sts.

With RS facing, rejoin yarn to rem sts, cast off centre 47 [47: 47: 47: 49: 49] sts, K to end.

Complete to match first side, reversing shapings.

FRONT

Work as given for back to ★★.

Dec 1 st at each end of next 7 [7: 9: 9: 11: 11] rows, then on foll 3 [3: 4: 2: 3: 3] alt rows. 97 [101: 101: 111: 115: 121] sts.

Work 1 row, ending with RS facing for next row.

Divide for front opening

Next row (RS): K2tog, K44 [46: 46: 51: 53: 56] and turn, leaving rem sts on a holder.

Work each side of neck separately.

Dec 1 st at armhole edge of 2nd [2nd: 0: 2nd: 2nd: 2nd] and foll 0 [0: 0: 2: 1: 2] alt rows. 44 [46: 47: 49: 52: 54] sts.

Cont straight until 31 [31: 31: 35: 35: 35] rows less have been worked than on back to beg of shoulder shaping, ending with **WS** facing for next row.

Shape neck

Cast off 11 [11: 11: 10: 11: 11] sts at beg of next row.

33 [35: 36: 39: 41: 43] sts.

Dec 1 st at neck edge of next 7 rows, then on foll 4 alt rows, then on 3 [3: 3: 4: 4: 4] foll 4th rows. 19 [21: 22: 24: 26: 28] sts.

Work 3 rows, ending with RS facing for next row.

Shape shoulder

Cast off 6 [7: 7: 8: 9: 9] sts at beg of next and foll alt row.

Work 1 row.

Cast off rem 7 [7: 8: 8: 8: 10] sts.

With RS facing, rejoin yarn to rem sts, cast off centre 5 sts, K to last 2 sts, K2tog.

41

Complete to match first side, reversing shapings.

SLEEVES

(handwritten: blauw 58 st)

Using 2¼mm (US 1) needles and yarn B cast on 77 [79: 81: 83: 85: 87] sts.
Row 1 (RS): K1 [2: 3: 1: 2: 3], *P1, K2, rep from * to last
1 [2: 3: 1: 2: 3] sts, P1, K0 [1: 2: 0: 1: 2].
Row 2: P1 [2: 3: 1: 2: 3], *K1, P2, rep from * to last 1 [2: 3: 1: 2: 3] sts,
K1, P0 [1: 2: 0: 1: 2].
These 2 rows form rib.
Keeping rib correct and joining in and breaking off colours as required,
work in stripes as folls:
Using yarn F, work 1 row. *(handwritten: wit)*
Using yarn B, work 3 rows. *(handwritten: BLAUW)*
Using yarn E, work 2 rows.
Using yarn B, work 4 rows, ending with RS facing for next row.
Break off yarns B and E and join in yarn D. *(handwritten: GROEN)*
Change to 2¾mm (US 2) needles.
Beg with a K row, work in st st, shaping sides by inc 1 st at each end of
next and every foll alt row until there are 105 [107: 109: 111: 113: 115] sts.
Work 3 rows, ending with RS facing for next row.

Shape top

Cast off 5 [6: 6: 7: 7: 8] sts at beg of next 2 rows.
95 [95: 97: 97: 99: 99] sts. *(handwritten: 95-18=77)*
Dec 1 st at each end of next 9 rows, then on every foll alt row until 63 sts
rem, then on foll 9 rows, ending with RS facing for next row. 45 sts.
Cast off 5 sts at beg of next 4 rows. *(handwritten: right sight)*
Cast off rem 25 sts.

MAKING UP

Press as described on the information page.

Join both shoulder seams using back stitch, or mattress stitch if preferred.

Button band

With RS facing, using 2¼mm (US 1) needles and yarn C, pick up and knit
31 sts evenly down left front opening edge, from neck shaping to base of
opening.
Row 1 (WS): K1, *P1, K1, rep from * to end.
Row 2: K2, *P1, K1, rep from * to last st, K1.
These 2 rows form rib.
Cont in rib for a further 3 rows, ending with RS facing for next row.
Cast off in rib.

Buttonhole band

With RS facing, using 2¼mm (US 1) needles and yarn C, pick up and knit
31 sts evenly up right front opening edge, from base of opening to neck
shaping.
Work in rib as given for button band for 5 rows, making buttonholes in
row 2 as folls:
Row 2 (RS): Rib 12, cast off 2 sts (to make first buttonhole – cast-on
2 sts over these cast-off sts on next row), rib until there are 12 sts on right
needle after cast-off, cast off 2 sts (to make 2nd buttonhole – cast-on 2 sts
over these cast-off sts on next row), rib to end.
When all 5 rows are complete, cast off in rib.

Collar

With RS facing, using 2¼mm (US 1) needles and yarn B, beg and ending
halfway across top of bands, pick up and knit
45 [45: 45: 48: 49: 49] sts up right side of neck, 55 [55: 55:
55: 57: 57] sts from back, then 45 [45: 45: 48: 49: 49] sts
down left side of neck. 145 [145: 145: 151: 155: 155] sts.
Row 1 (RS of collar, WS of body): K2 [2: 2: 5: 3: 3], inc in next st,
(K3, inc in next st) 35 [35: 35: 35: 37: 37] times,
K to end. 181 [181: 181: 187: 193: 193] sts.

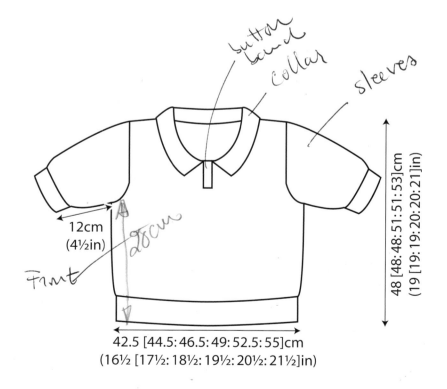

(handwritten labels: button band, collar, sleeves)

12cm
(4½in)

(handwritten: 20cm)

(handwritten: Front)

48 [48: 48: 51: 51: 53]cm
(19 [19: 19: 20: 20: 21]in)

42.5 [44.5: 46.5: 49: 52.5: 55]cm
(16½ [17½: 18½: 19½: 20½: 21½]in)

(handwritten: Florien : 34 cm)

Row 1 (WS of collar): K1, ★P2, K1, rep from ★ to end.
Row 2: K3, ★P1, K2, rep from ★ to last st, K1.
These 2 rows form rib.
Keeping rib correct, cont as folls:
Rows 3 and 4: Rib to last 57 sts, wrap next st (by slipping next st from left needle to right needle, taking yarn to opposite side of work between needles and then slipping same st back onto left needle – when working back across wrapped sts, work the wrapped st and the wrapping loop tog as one st) and turn.
Rows 5 and 6: Rib to last 45 sts, wrap next st and turn.
Rows 7 and 8: Rib to last 33 sts, wrap next st and turn.
Rows 9 and 10: Rib to last 21 sts, wrap next st and turn.
Row 11: Rib to end.
Now working in rib across all sts, cont in rib until collar meas 9 cm **at centre back neck** from pick-up row, ending with RS of collar facing for next row.
Join in yarn E.
Using yarn E, work 2 rows.
Using yarn B, work 3 rows.
Using yarn E, work 1 row.
Break off yarn E and cont using yarn B only.
Work in rib for a further 2 rows, ending with RS of collar facing for next row.
Cast off in rib.
Front opening trim
With **WS** facing, using 2.50mm (US C2) crochet hook and yarn D, attach yarn at end of cast-off edge of buttonhole band, 1 ch (does NOT count as st), work 17 dc evenly down cast-off edge to beg of cast-off edge, turn.
Next row (RS): 1 ch (does NOT count as st), 1 dc into first dc, ★miss 1 dc, 5 tr into next dc, miss 1 dc, 1 dc into next dc, rep from ★ to end.

Fasten off.
Lay buttonhole band over button band and sew row-end edges of bands to cast-off sts at base of opening.
See information page for finishing instructions, setting in sleeves using the set-in method.
Hem trim
With **WS** facing, using 2.50mm (US C2) crochet hook and yarn D, attach yarn at base of one side seam, 1 ch (does NOT count as st), work 1 round of dc evenly around entire cast-on edge of back and front, working approx 1 dc into each cast-on st and ensuring total number of dc worked is divisible by 4, ss to first dc, turn.
Next round (RS): 1 ch (does NOT count as st), 1 dc into first dc, ★miss 1 dc, 5 tr into next dc, miss 1 dc, 1 dc into next dc, rep from ★ to end, replacing dc at end of last rep with ss to first dc.
Fasten off.
Sleeve trim
With **WS** facing, using 2.50mm (US C2) crochet hook and yarn D, attach yarn at base of sleeve seam, 1 ch (does NOT count as st), work 1 round of dc evenly around entire cast-on edge, working approx 1 dc into each cast-on st and ensuring total number of dc worked is divisible by 4, ss to first dc, turn.
Next round (RS): 1 ch (does NOT count as st), 1 dc into first dc, ★miss 1 dc, 5 tr into next dc, miss 1 dc, 1 dc into next dc, rep from ★ to end, replacing dc at end of last rep with ss to first dc.
Fasten off.
Using photograph as a guide, embroider bullion knots onto patt rows 5 to 11 of back and front as folls: For first band of knots, use yarn C for knots on the K sts, and yarn E for knots on P sts. For second band of knots, use yarn C for knots on the K sts, and yarn D for knots on P sts. For 3rd band of knots, use yarn C for knots on the K sts, and yarn B for knots on P sts.

YARN

	S	M	L	XL	XXL	
To fit bust						
	81-86	91-97	102-107	112-117	122-127	cm
	32-34	36-38	40-42	44-46	48-50	in
Rowan Milk Cotton DK						
A Black Jacks 101						
	6	7	7	8	8	x 50gm
B Liquorice 099						
	8	8	9	10	10	x 50gm

NEEDLES

1 pair 3¼mm (no 10) (US 3) needles
1 pair 3¾mm (no 9) (US 5) needles
3¼mm (no 10) (US 3) circular needle

TENSION

22 sts and 30 rows to 10 cm measured over st st using 3¾mm (US 5) needles.

Bailey

BACK and FRONT (both alike)
Using 3¼mm (US 3) needles and yarn A cast on 129 [142: 161: 180: 198] sts.
Beg with a K row, work in st st as folls:
Using yarn A, work 4 rows.
Join in yarn B.
Using yarn B, work 12 rows.
Change to 3¾mm (US 5) needles.
Cont in striped st st as folls:
Rows 1 to 4: Using yarn A.
Row 5: Using yarn B.
These 5 rows form striped st st.
Cont in striped st st until work meas approx 38 [39: 40: 41: 42] cm
allowing first few rows to roll to RS, ending after 2 or 3 rows using yarn
A and with **WS** facing for next row.
Next row (WS): Using yarn A, P1 [2: 1: 1: 2], (P2tog, P2)
31 [34: 39: 44: 48] times, P2tog, P2 [2: 2: 1: 2].
Cast off rem 97 [107: 121: 135: 149] sts.

YOKE (worked sideways from cuff to cuff)
Using 3¼mm (US 3) needles and yarn B cast on 88 [90: 92: 92: 94] sts.
Beg with a K row, work in st st as folls:
Using yarn B, work 4 rows.
Join in yarn A.
Using yarn A, work 12 rows.
Change to 3¾mm (US 5) needles.
Cont in striped st st as folls:
Row 1: Using yarn B, inc in first st, K to last st, inc in last st.
90 [92: 94: 94: 96] sts.
Rows 2 to 4: Using yarn B.
Row 5: Using yarn A, (inc in first st) 0 [0: 0: 1: 1] times, K to last 0 [0: 0:
1: 1] sts, (inc in last st) 0 [0: 0: 1: 1] times.
90 [92: 94: 96: 98] sts.
These 5 rows form striped st st and beg sleeve shaping.
Cont in striped st st, shaping sides by inc 1 st at each end of
2nd [2nd: 2nd: 4th: 4th] and every foll 6th [6th: 6th: 4th: 4th] row to
118 [126: 132: 106: 114] sts, then on every foll 8th [8th: –: 6th: 6th] row
until there are 124 [128: –: 136: 140] sts.
Work 11 rows, ending after 1 [2: 1: 1: 1] row using yarn A [B: B:

B: B] and with RS facing for next row.
Place markers at both ends of last row to denote top of sleeve seam.
Work 37 [45: 49: 59: 67] rows, ending after 2 [2: 1: 1: 3] rows using yarn
B [B: A: A: B] and with **WS** facing for next row.
Divide for neck
Keeping stripes correct, cont as folls:
Next row (WS): P60 [62: 64: 66: 68], P2tog and turn, leaving rem sts on
a holder.
Work each side of neck separately.
Dec 1 st at neck edge of next 3 rows. 58 [60: 62: 64: 66] sts.
Work 53 [53: 57: 57: 61] rows, ending after 4 [4: 1: 1: 3] rows using yarn B
and with RS facing for next row.
Inc 1 st at neck edge of next 3 rows, ending with **WS** facing for next row.
61 [63: 65: 67: 69] sts.
Break yarns and leave sts on a holder.
With **WS** facing, rejoin yarns to rem sts, P2tog, P to end.
Dec 1 st at neck edge of next 3 rows. 58 [60: 62: 64: 66] sts.
Work 53 [53: 57: 57: 61] rows, ending after 4 [4: 1: 1: 3] rows using yarn B
and with RS facing for next row.
Inc 1 st at neck edge of next 3 rows, ending with **WS** facing for next row.
61 [63: 65: 67: 69] sts.
Break yarns.
Join sections
Next row (WS): P to last st of first section, inc in last st, inc in first st of
second section, P to end. 124 [128: 132: 136: 140] sts.
Work 36 [44: 48: 58: 66] rows, ending after 4 [2: 3: 3: 3] rows using yarn B
and with RS facing for next row.
Place markers at both ends of last row to denote top of other sleeve seam.
Work 12 rows, ending with RS facing for next row.
Dec 1 st at each end of next and every foll 8th [8th: 6th: 6th: 6th] row to
116 [124: 94: 104: 112] sts, then on every foll 6th [6th: –: 4th: 4th] row until
90 [92: –: 94: 96] sts rem.
Work 5 [5: 5: 3: 3] rows, ending after 4 rows using yarn B and with RS
facing for next row.
Change to 3¼mm (US 3) needles.
Using yarn A, work in st st for 12 rows, dec 1 st at each end of first of these
rows and ending with RS facing for next row.
Using yarn B, work 4 rows, ending with RS facing for next row.
Cast off.

44

MAKING UP
Press as described on the information page.
Neckband
With RS facing, using 3¼mm (US 3) circular needle and yarn B, beg and ending at dividing row of neck shaping, pick up and knit 50 [50: 53: 53: 56] sts along one row-end edge of neck shaping to joining row, then 50 [50: 53: 53: 56] sts along other row-end edge of neck shaping back to starting point. 100 [100: 106: 106: 112] sts.

Cast off purlwise (on RS).

Sew cast-off edges of back and front to yoke between markers. See information page for finishing instructions, reversing seams for first 4 rows (and last 4 rows of yoke) for st st roll.

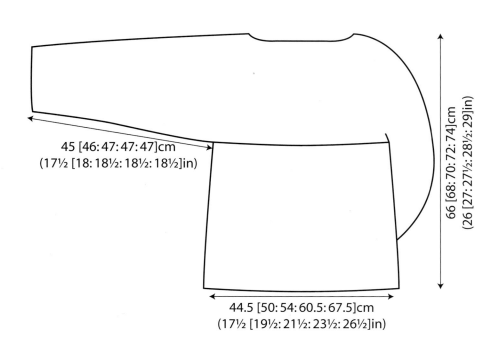

45 [46: 47: 47: 47]cm
(17½ [18: 18½: 18½: 18½]in)

66 [68: 70: 72: 74]cm
(26 [27: 27½: 28½: 29]in)

44.5 [50: 54: 60.5: 67.5]cm
(17½ [19½: 21½: 23½: 26½]in)

Jocelynn ••

YARN

		8	10	12	14	16	18	20	22	
To fit bust		81	86	91	97	102	107	112	117	cm
		32	34	36	38	40	42	44	46	in
Rowan Milk Cotton DK										
A Scented Satin	088	2	2	2	2	2	2	2	3	x 50gm
B Water Bomb	098	1	1	1	1	2	2	2	2	x 50gm
C Barley Sugar	081	1	1	1	1	1	1	1	1	x 50gm
D Midget Gem	097	1	1	1	1	1	1	1	1	x 50gm
E Bonfire Toffee	091	1	1	1	1	1	1	1	1	x 50gm
F Aniseed	090	1	1	1	1	2	2	2	2	x 50gm
G Liquorice	099	1	1	1	1	1	1	1	2	x 50gm
H Curly Wurly	100	1	1	1	1	1	1	1	1	x 50gm
I Jelly Baby	096	1	1	1	1	1	1	1	1	x 50gm

NEEDLES
1 pair 3¼mm (no 10) (US 3) needles & 1 pair 3¾mm (no 9) (US 5) needles

BUTTONS – 2 x BN1028

TENSION
22 sts and 30 rows to 10 cm measured over st st using 3¾mm (US 5) needles

STRIPE SEQUENCE

Rows 1 to 4: Using yarn B.
Row 5: Using yarn C.
Rows 6 to 8: Using yarn D.
Rows 9 to 12: Using yarn E.
Rows 13 to 15: Using yarn D.
Row 16: Using yarn C.
Rows 17 to 20: Using yarn B.
Row 21: Using yarn C.
Row 22: Using yarn F.
Rows 23 to 25: Using yarn G.
Rows 26 to 29: Using yarn A.
Rows 30 to 32: Using yarn G.
Row 33: Using yarn F.
Rows 34 and 35: Using yarn H.
Row 36: Using yarn F.
Rows 37 and 38: Using yarn I.
Rows 39 to 42: Using yarn F.
Rows 43 and 44: Using yarn I.
Row 45: Using yarn F.
Rows 46 and 47: Using yarn H.
Row 48: Using yarn F.
Row 49: Using yarn C.

These 49 rows form stripe sequence and are repeated throughout. Note that on first and 3rd rep of stripe sequence, odd numbered rows are knit rows, but on 2nd (and 4th) rep, odd numbered rows are **purl** rows.

BACK

Using 3¼mm (US 3) needles and yarn A cast on 93 [97: 101: 107: 115: 121: 127: 135] sts.
Work in g st for 3 rows, ending with RS facing for next row.
Change to 3¾mm (US 5) needles.
Beg with a K row, work in st st in stripe sequence as given above as folls:
Work 4 rows, ending with RS facing for next row.
Dec 1 st at each end of next and 4 foll 4th rows.
83 [87: 91: 97: 105: 111: 117: 125] sts.
Work 11 rows, ending with RS facing for next row.
Inc 1 st at each end of next and every foll 8th row until there are

93 [97: 101: 107: 115: 121: 127: 135] sts.★★
Cont straight until back meas 29 [29: 28: 31: 30: 32: 31: 33] cm, ending with RS facing for next row.

Shape armholes
Keeping stripes correct, cast off 4 [5: 5: 6: 6: 7: 7: 8] sts at beg of next 2 rows. 85 [87: 91: 95: 103: 107: 113: 119] sts.
Dec 1 st at each end of next 5 [5: 7: 7: 9: 9: 11: 11] rows, then on foll 6 [5: 4: 5: 5: 5: 5: 6] alt rows. 63 [67: 69: 71: 75: 79: 81: 85] sts.
Cont straight until armhole meas 18 [18: 19: 19: 20: 20: 21: 21] cm, ending with RS facing for next row.

Shape shoulders and back neck
Next row (RS): Cast off 4 [5: 6: 6: 7: 8: 8: 9] sts, K until there are 8 [9: 9: 10: 10: 11: 12: 13] sts on right needle and turn, leaving rem sts on a holder.
Work each side of neck separately.
Cast off 3 sts at beg of next row.
Cast off rem 5 [6: 6: 7: 7: 8: 9: 10] sts.
With RS facing, rejoin yarns to rem sts, cast off centre 39 [39: 39: 39: 41: 41: 41: 41] sts, K to end.
Complete to match first side, reversing shapings.

FRONT

Work as given for back to ★★.
Cont straight until 14 [14: 12: 16: 12: 12: 12: 12] rows less have been worked than on back to beg of armhole shaping, ending with RS facing for next row.

Divide for front opening
Next row (RS): K45 [47: 49: 52: 56: 59: 62: 66] and turn, leaving rem sts on a holder.
Work each side of neck separately.
Work 13 [13: 11: 15: 11: 11: 11: 11] rows, ending with RS facing for next row.

Shape armhole
Keeping stripes correct, cast off 4 [5: 5: 6: 6: 7: 7: 8] sts at beg of next row.
41 [42: 44: 46: 50: 52: 55: 58] sts.
Work 1 row.
Dec 1 st at armhole edge of next 5 [5: 7: 6: 9: 9: 10: 10] rows, then on foll 1 [1: 1: 0: 0: 0: 0: 0] alt rows. 35 [36: 36: 40: 41: 43: 45: 48] sts.
Work 1 [1: 1: 0: 1: 1: 0: 0] row, ending with RS facing for next row.

Shape neck

Next row (RS): K2tog, K24 [25: 25: 29: 29: 31: 33: 36], cast off rem 9 [9: 9: 9: 9: 10: 10: 10: 10] sts. 25 [26: 26: 30: 30: 32: 34: 37] sts.

Keeping stripes correct, dec 1 st at neck edge of next 8 rows, then on foll 2 alt rows, then on foll 4th row, then on foll 6th row **and at same time** dec 1 st at armhole edge of 2nd and foll 3 [2: 1: 4: 3: 3: 4: 5] alt rows. 9 [11: 12: 13: 14: 16: 17: 19] sts.

Cont straight until front matches back to beg of shoulder shaping, ending with RS facing for next row.

Shape shoulder

Cast off 4 [5: 6: 6: 7: 8: 8: 9] sts at beg of next row.

Work 1 row.

Cast off rem 5 [6: 6: 7: 7: 8: 9: 10] sts.

With RS facing, rejoin appropriate yarn to rem sts, cast off centre 3 sts, K to end.

Complete to match first side, reversing shapings.

SLEEVES

Using 3¼mm (US 3) needles and yarn H cast on 77 [79: 81: 83: 85: 87: 89: 91] sts.

Work in g st for 3 rows, ending with RS facing for next row.

Break off yarn H and join in yarn A.

Change to 3¾mm (US 5) needles.

Beg with a K row, work in st st as folls:

Shape top

Cast off 4 [5: 5: 6: 6: 7: 7: 8] sts at beg of next 2 rows. 69 [69: 71: 71: 73: 73: 75: 75] sts.

Dec 1 st at each end of next 5 rows, then on every foll alt row until 53 sts rem, then on foll 5 rows, ending with RS facing for next row. 43 sts.

Cast off 6 sts at beg of next 4 rows.

Cast off rem 19 sts.

MAKING UP

Press as described on the information page.

Join both shoulder seams using back stitch, or mattress stitch if preferred.

Button band

With RS facing, using 3¼mm (US 3) needles and yarn B, pick up and knit 18 sts evenly down left front opening edge, from neck shaping to base of opening.

Beg with a P row, work in st st for 4 rows, ending with **WS** facing for next row.

Cast off knitwise (on **WS**).

Buttonhole band

With RS facing, using 3¼mm (US 3) needles and yarn B, pick up and knit 18 sts evenly up right front opening edge, from base of opening to neck shaping.

Row 1 (WS): Purl.

Row 2: (K6, yfwd, K2tog) twice, K2.

Beg with a P row, work in st st for 2 rows, ending with **WS** facing for next row.

Cast off knitwise (on **WS**).

Lay buttonhole band over button band and sew row-end edges of bands to cast-off sts at base of opening.

Neckband

With RS facing, using 3¼mm (US 3) needles and yarn A, beg and ending at cast-off edge of bands, pick up and knit 60 [60: 60: 64: 65: 65: 67: 67] sts up right side of neck, 45 [45: 45: 45: 47: 47: 47: 47] sts from back, then 60 [60: 60: 64: 65: 65: 67: 67] sts down left side of neck. 165 [165: 165: 173: 177: 177: 181: 181] sts.

Work in g st for 2 rows, ending with **WS** facing for next row.

Cast off knitwise (on **WS**).

Front insert (optional)

Using 3¾mm (US 5) needles and yarn I cast on 21 [21: 21: 21: 23: 23: 23: 23] sts.

Beg with a K row, work in st st, inc 1 st at each end of 2nd and foll 7 rows, then on foll 2 alt rows. 41 [41: 41: 41: 43: 43: 43: 43] sts.

Work 3 rows, ending with RS facing for next row.

Break off yarn I and join in yarn D.

Change to 3¼mm (US 3) needles.

Work in g st for 3 rows, ending with **WS** facing for next row.

Cast off knitwise (on **WS**).

See information page for finishing instructions, setting in sleeves using the set-in method. Sew front insert into neck shaping, matching row-end and cast-on edges to neckband pick-up row.

Sew on buttons.

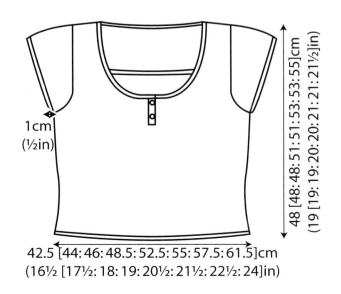

1cm (½in)

48 [48: 48: 51: 51: 53: 53: 55]cm (19 [19: 19: 20: 20: 21: 21: 21½]in)

42.5 [44: 46: 48.5: 52.5: 55: 57.5: 61.5]cm (16½ [17½: 18: 19: 20½: 21½: 22½: 24]in)

YARN

	8	10	12	14	16	18	
To fit bust							
	81	86	91	97	102	107	cm
	32	34	36	38	40	42	in

Rowan Fine Milk Cotton

			8	10	12	14	16	18		
A	Jelly Baby	496	8	9	9	10	10	11	x	50gm
B	Water Bomb	498	1	1	1	1	1	1	x	50gm

NEEDLES

1 pair 2mm (no 14) (US 0) needles
1 pair 2¾mm (no 12) (US 2) needles
Cable needle
2.50mm (no 12) (US C2) crochet hook

BUTTONS – 1 x BN1152

TENSION

30 sts and 38 rows to 10 cm measured over st st using 2¾mm (US 2) needles.

UK CROCHET ABBREVIATIONS

ch = chain; **dc** = double crochet.

BACK

Using 2mm (US 0) needles and yarn B cast on 166 [172: 178: 188: 196: 206] sts.

Row 1 (WS): Knit.

Break off yarn B and join in yarn A.

Change to 2¾mm (US 2) needles.

Beg with a K row, work in st st, dec 1 st at each end of 11th and every foll 6th row until 154 [160: 166: 176: 184: 194] sts rem.

Work 1 row, ending with RS facing for next row.

Row 43 (RS): K10 [10: 10: 12: 13: 15], ★slip next 5 sts on left needle onto right needle, then slip foll 10 sts from left needle onto cable needle, slip 5 sts now on right needle back onto left needle keeping cable needle at back of work, K tog first st on left needle with first st on cable needle, (K tog next st on left needle with next st on cable needle) 9 times★★, K18 [20: 22: 24: 26: 28], rep from ★ twice more, then from ★ to ★★ again, K10 [10: 10: 12: 13: 15].

114 [120: 126: 136: 144: 154] sts.

Work 1 row.

Row 45 (eyelet row) (RS): K4 [2: 5: 5: 4: 4], ★yfwd, K2tog, K3, rep from ★ to last 5 [3: 6: 6: 5: 5] sts, yfwd, K2tog, K3 [1: 4: 4: 3: 3].

Beg with a P row, cont in st st, inc 1 st at each end of 10th and every foll 10th row until there are 126 [132: 138: 148: 156: 166] sts.

Cont straight until back meas 32 [32: 31: 34: 33: 35] cm, ending with RS facing for next row.

Shape armholes

Cast off 5 [6: 6: 7: 7: 8] sts at beg of next 2 rows.

116 [120: 126: 134: 142: 150] sts.

Dec 1 st at each end of next 7 [7: 9: 9: 11: 11] rows, then on foll 4 [5: 4: 6: 6: 8] alt rows. 94 [96: 100: 104: 108: 112] sts.★★★

Cont straight until armhole meas 11 [11: 12: 12: 13: 13] cm, ending with RS facing for next row.

Divide for back opening

Next row (RS): K47 [48: 50: 52: 54: 56] and turn, leaving rem sts on a holder.

Work each side of neck separately.

Next row (WS): K1, P to end.

Next row: Knit.

These 2 rows set the sts – back opening edge st now worked as a K st on every row with all other sts still in st st.

Keeping sts correct as now set, cont straight until armhole meas 18 [18: 19: 19: 20: 20] cm, ending with RS facing for next row.

Shape shoulder and back neck

Cast off 8 [8: 9: 9: 9: 10] sts at beg of next row, 20 [20: 20: 20: 22: 22] sts at beg of foll row, 8 [8: 9: 9: 9: 10] sts at beg of next row, then 4 sts at beg of foll row.

Cast off rem 7 [8: 8: 10: 10: 10] sts.

With RS facing, rejoin yarn to rem sts, K to end.

Next row (WS): P to last st, K1.

Next row: Knit.

These 2 rows set the sts – back opening edge st now worked as a K st on every row with all other sts still in st st.

Keeping sts correct as now set, complete to match first side, reversing shapings.

FRONT

Work as given for back to ★★★.

Cont straight until 32 [32: 32: 36: 36: 36] rows less have been worked than on back to beg of shoulder shaping, ending with RS facing for next row.

Shape neck

Next row (RS): K38 [39: 41: 44: 44: 46] and turn, leaving rem sts on a holder.

Work each side of neck separately.

Dec 1 st at neck edge of next 8 rows, then on foll 4 alt rows, then on 3 [3: 3: 4: 4: 4] foll 4th rows. 23 [24: 26: 28: 28: 30] sts.

Work 3 rows, ending with RS facing for next row.

Shape shoulder

Cast off 8 [8: 9: 9: 9: 10] sts at beg of next and foll alt row.

Work 1 row.

Cast off rem 7 [8: 8: 10: 10: 10] sts.

With RS facing, rejoin yarn to rem sts, cast off centre 18 [18: 18: 16: 20: 20] sts, K to end.

Complete to match first side, reversing shapings.

SLEEVES

Using 2mm (US 0) needles and yarn B cast on 60 [60: 64: 64: 66: 66] sts.

Row 1 (WS): Knit.

Break off yarn B and join in yarn A.
Change to 2¾mm (US 2) needles.
Beg with a K row, work in st st, shaping sides by inc 1 st at each end of 5th and every foll 6th row to 92 [100: 92: 100: 98: 106] sts, then on every foll 8th row until there are 106 [108: 110: 112: 114: 116] sts.
Cont straight until sleeve meas 45 [45: 46: 46: 47: 47] cm, ending with RS facing for next row.

Shape top
Cast off 5 [6: 6: 7: 7: 8] sts at beg of next 2 rows.
96 [96: 98: 98: 100: 100] sts.
Dec 1 st at each end of next and every alt row until 88 sts rem.
Work 1 row, ending with RS facing for next row.
Cast off 4 sts at beg of next 16 rows.
Cast off rem 24 sts.

MAKING UP
Press as described on the information page.
Join both shoulder seams using back stitch, or mattress stitch if preferred.

Neckband
With RS facing, using 2mm (US 0) needles and yarn B, beg and ending at top of back opening, pick up and knit 24 [24: 24: 24: 26: 26] sts from left back neck edge, 32 [32: 32: 36: 36: 36] sts down left side of neck, 18 [18: 18: 16: 20: 20] sts from front, 32 [32: 32: 36: 36: 36] sts up right side of neck, then 24 [24: 24: 24: 26: 26] sts from right back neck edge.
130 [130: 130: 136: 144: 144] sts.
Cast off knitwise (on **WS**).
See information page for finishing instructions, setting in sleeves using the set-in method. Make a button loop at one end of neckband and attach button to other end of neckband to fasten back neck opening.

Tie
Using 2.50mm (US C2) crochet hook and yarn B, make a ch approx 120 [120: 130: 130: 140: 140] cm long.
Row 1: 1 dc into 2nd ch from hook, 1 dc into each ch to end.
Fasten off.
Thread tie through eyelet row at waist and tie ends in a bow at centre front.

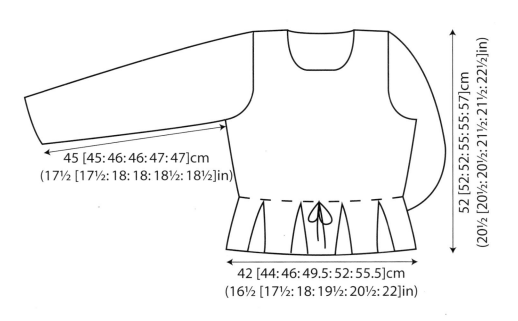

45 [45: 46: 46: 47: 47]cm
(17½ [17½: 18: 18: 18½: 18½]in)

52 [52: 52: 55: 55: 57]cm
(20½ [20½: 20½: 21½: 21½: 22½]in)

42 [44: 46: 49.5: 52: 55.5]cm
(16½ [17½: 18: 19½: 20½: 22]in)

Magda

YARN

	S	M	L	XL	XXL	
To fit bust						
	81-86	91-97	102-107	112-117	122-127	cm
	32-34	36-38	40-42	44-46	48-50	in
Rowan Milk Cotton DK						
	13	14	16	17	19	x 50gm

(photographed in Pastille 094)

NEEDLES

1 pair 3mm (no 11) (US 2/3) needles
1 pair 3¼mm (no 10) (US 3) needles
2¾mm (no 12) (US 2) circular needle

BUTTONS – 1 x BN1089

TENSION

23 sts and 34 rows to 10 cm measured over st st using 3¼mm (US 3) needles.

LOWER BACK
Using 3mm (US 2/3) needles cast on 133 [149: 169: 187: 209] sts.
Work in g st for 36 rows, ending with RS facing for next row.
Change to 3¼mm (US 3) needles.
Beg with a K row, work in st st until lower back meas 26 [27: 28: 29: 30] cm, ending with **WS** facing for next row.
Next row (WS): P3 [3: 1: 2: 1], (P2tog, P2) 31 [35: 41: 45: 51] times, P2tog, P4 [4: 2: 3: 2].
Cast off rem 101 [113: 127: 141: 157] sts.

LOWER FRONTS (both alike)
Using 3mm (US 2/3) needles cast on 53 [61: 69: 79: 89] sts.
Work in g st for 36 rows, ending with RS facing for next row.
Change to 3¼mm (US 3) needles.
Beg with a K row, work in st st until lower front meas 26 [27: 28: 29: 30] cm, ending with **WS** facing for next row.
Next row (WS): P1 [1: 3: 2: 3], (P2tog, P2) 12 [14: 15: 18: 20] times, P2tog, P2 [2: 4: 3: 4].
Cast off rem 40 [46: 53: 60: 68] sts.

LEFT SLEEVE AND YOKE (worked sideways beg at cuff)
Using 3mm (US 2/3) needles cast on 92 [94: 96: 96: 98] sts.
Work in g st for 36 rows, ending with RS facing for next row.
Change to 3¼mm (US 3) needles.
Beg with a K row, work in st st, shaping sides by inc 1 st at each end of 5th [3rd: 3rd: 3rd: 3rd] and every foll 6th [4th: 4th: 4th: 4th] row to 128 [102: 106: 118: 132] sts, then on every foll - [6th: 6th: 6th: 6th] row until there are - [134: 138: 142: 148] sts.
Cont straight until this sleeve section meas 45 [46: 47: 47: 47] cm, ending with RS facing for next row.
Place markers at both ends of last row to denote top of sleeve seam.
Work 42 [50: 58: 68: 78] rows, ending with RS facing for next row.
Divide for back and front neck
Next row (RS): K64 [67: 69: 71: 74] and turn, leaving rem sts on a holder.
Work each side of neck separately.
Dec 1 st at neck edge of beg of next row and at same edge on foll 2 rows. 61 [64: 66: 68: 71] sts.
Work 30 [30: 32: 32: 34] rows, ending with RS facing for next row.
Cast off. (This cast-off edge forms centre back seam of yoke.)
With RS facing, rejoin yarn to rem sts, cast off 8 [8: 7: 7: 7] sts, K to end. 56 [59: 62: 64: 67] sts.
Work 1 row.
Cast off 8 [8: 7: 8: 7] sts at beg of next and foll 5 [3: 1: 6: 4] alt rows, then

0 [9: 8: 0: 8] sts at beg of foll 0 [2: 5: 0: 3] alt rows.
Work 1 row, ending with RS facing for next row.
Cast off rem 8 [9: 8: 8: 8] sts.

RIGHT SLEEVE AND YOKE (worked sideways beg at cuff)
Work to match left sleeve and yoke, reversing shapings.

MAKING UP
Press as described on the information page.
Join centre back seam of yoke sections using back stitch, or mattress stitch if preferred. Sew lower back to joined yoke sections between markers, matching centre of lower back cast-off edge to centre back yoke seam. Sew lower fronts to row-end edges of front sections of yoke from marker to final cast-off edge.
Front band
With RS facing and using 2¾mm (US 2) circular needle, beg and ending at lower front cast-on edges, pick up and knit 60 [62: 64: 67: 69] sts up row-end edge of lower right front to yoke seam, 74 [76: 79: 81: 84] sts up shaped cast-off edge of right front slope to yoke dividing point, 46 [46: 49: 49: 51] sts from back neck to dividing point of other yoke section,
74 [76: 79: 81: 84] sts down shaped cast-off edge of left front slope to yoke seam, then 60 [62: 64: 67: 69] sts down row-end edge of lower left front. 314 [322: 335: 345: 357] sts.
Work in g st for 10 rows, ending with **WS** facing for next row.
Row 11 (WS): K to last 61 [63: 65: 68: 70] sts, cast off 2 sts (to make a buttonhole – cast on 2 sts over these cast-off sts on next row), K to end.
Work in g st for a further 11 rows, ending with **WS** facing for next row.
Cast off knitwise (on **WS**).
See information page for finishing instructions.

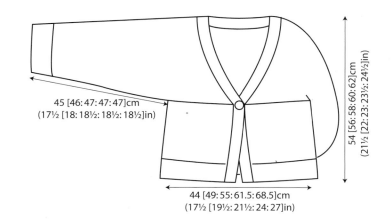

45 [46: 47: 47: 47]cm
(17½ [18: 18½: 18½: 18½]in)

54 [56: 58: 60: 62]cm
(21½ [22: 23: 23½: 24½]in)

44 [49: 55: 61.5: 68.5]cm
(17½ [19½: 21½: 24: 27]in)

YARN

	S	M	L	XL	XXL	
To fit bust						
	81-86	91-97	102-107	112-117	122-127	cm
	32-34	36-38	40-42	44-46	48-50	in

Rowan Milk Cotton DK
A Black Jacks 101

	3	3	4	4	4	x 50gm

B Curly Wurly 100

	9	10	11	12	13	x 50gm

NEEDLES

1 pair 3¼mm (no 10) (US 3) needles

TENSION

30 sts and 34 rows to 10 cm measured over rib when slightly stretched using 3¼mm (US 3) needles.

Abigail

BACK

Using 3¼mm (US 3) needles and yarn A cast on 134 [150: 166: 186: 206] sts.
Row 1 (RS): K2, *P2, K2, rep from * to end.
Row 2: P2, *K2, P2, rep from * to end.
These 2 rows form rib.
Cont in rib, dec 1 st at each end of 7th and 5 foll 6th rows.
122 [138: 154: 174: 194] sts.
Work 1 row, ending with RS facing for next row.
Break off yarn A and join in yarn B.
Cont in rib, inc 1 st at each end of 9th and every foll 10th row until there are 134 [150: 166: 186: 206] sts, taking inc sts into rib.
Cont straight until back meas 32 [33: 34: 35: 36] cm, ending with RS facing for next row.
Shape armholes
Cast off 7 [8: 9: 10: 11] sts at beg of next 2 rows.
120 [134: 148: 166: 184] sts.
Dec 1 st at each end of next 9 [9: 11: 11: 13] rows, then on foll 3 [7: 7: 12: 14] alt rows. 96 [102: 112: 120: 130] sts.
Cont straight until armhole meas 18 [19: 20: 21: 22] cm, ending with RS facing for next row.
Shape shoulders and back neck
Cast off 7 [8: 9: 10: 12] sts at beg of next 2 rows.
82 [86: 94: 100: 106] sts.
Next row (RS): Cast off 7 [8: 9: 10: 12] sts, rib until there are 11 [12: 13: 15: 15] sts on right needle and turn, leaving rem sts on a holder.
Work each side of neck separately.
Cast off 4 sts at beg of next row.
Cast off rem 7 [8: 9: 11: 11] sts.
With RS facing, rejoin yarn to rem sts, cast off centre 46 [46: 50: 50: 52] sts, rib to end.
Complete to match first side, reversing shapings.

FRONT

Work as given for back until 28 [28: 30: 30: 32] rows less have been worked than on back to beg of shoulder shaping, ending with RS facing for next row.
Shape neck
Next row (RS): Rib 36 [39: 43: 47: 52] and turn, leaving rem sts on a holder.
Work each side of neck separately.
Dec 1 st at neck edge of next 8 rows, then on foll 6 [6: 7: 7: 8] alt rows, then on foll 4th row. 21 [24: 27: 31: 35] sts.
Work 3 rows, ending with RS facing for next row.
Shape shoulder
Cast off 7 [8: 9: 10: 12] sts at beg of next and foll alt row.
Work 1 row.
Cast off rem 7 [8: 9: 11: 11] sts.
With RS facing, rejoin yarn to rem sts, cast off centre 24 [24: 26: 26: 26] sts,

rib to end.
Complete to match first side, reversing shapings.

SLEEVES

Using 3¼mm (US 3) needles and yarn A cast on 62 [66: 70: 70: 74] sts.
Work in rib as given for back until sleeve meas 10 cm, ending with RS facing for next row.
Break off yarn A and join in yarn B.
Cont in rib, shaping sides by inc 1 st at each end of 3rd and every foll 4th row to 74 [74: 76: 88: 92] sts, then on every foll 6th row until there are 108 [112: 116: 120: 124] sts, taking inc sts into rib.
Cont straight until sleeve meas 52 [53: 54: 54: 54] cm, ending with RS facing for next row.
Shape top
Cast off 7 [8: 9: 10: 11] sts at beg of next 2 rows.
94 [96: 98: 100: 102] sts.
Cast off 3 [3: 3: 2: 2] sts at beg of next 8 [14: 20: 2: 6] rows, then 4 [4: 4: 3: 3] sts at beg of foll 10 [6: 2: 22: 20] rows.
Cast off rem 30 sts.

MAKING UP

Press as described on the information page.
Join right shoulder seam using back stitch, or mattress stitch if preferred.
Neckband
With RS facing, using 3¼mm (US 3) needles and yarn B, pick up and knit 28 [28: 30: 30: 32] sts down left side of neck, 24 [24: 26: 26: 26] sts from front, 28 [28: 30: 30: 32] sts up right side of neck, then 54 [54: 58: 58: 60] sts from back.
134 [134: 144: 144: 150] sts.
Cast off knitwise (on **WS**).
See information page for finishing instructions, setting in sleeves using the set-in method.

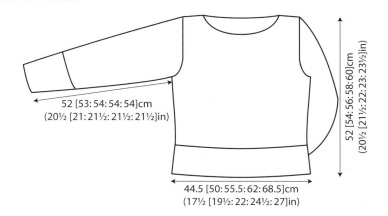

52 [53: 54: 54: 54]cm
(20½ [21: 21½: 21½: 21½]in)

52 [54: 56: 58: 60]cm
(20½ [21½: 22: 23: 23½]in)

44.5 [50: 55.5: 62: 68.5]cm
(17½ [19½: 22: 24½: 27]in)

YARN

	S	M	L	XL	XXL	
To fit bust	81-86	91-97	102-107	112-117	122-127	cm
	32-34	36-38	40-42	44-46	48-50	in
Rowan Milk Cotton DK	8	9	10	11	12	x 50gm

(photographed in Liquorice 099)

NEEDLES – 1 pair 3¼mm (no 10) (US 3) needles, 1 pair 3¾mm (no 9) (US 5) needles & Cable needle

BUTTONS – 4 x BN1116

TENSION – 30 sts and 30 rows to 10 cm measured over patt using 3¾mm (US 5) needles.

SPECIAL ABBREVIATIONS

Cr3R = slip next st onto cable needle and leave at back of work, K2, then P1 from cable needle; **Cr3L** = slip next 2 sts onto cable needle and leave at front of work, P1, then K2 from cable needle; **C4B** = slip next 2 sts onto cable needle and leave at back of work, K2, then K2 from cable needle; **C4F** = slip next 2 sts onto cable needle and leave at front of work, K2, then K2 from cable needle; **Cr4R** = slip next 2 sts onto cable needle and leave at back of work, K2, then P2 from cable needle; **Cr4L** = slip next 2 sts onto cable needle and leave at front of work, P2, then K2 from cable needle; **C6B** = slip next 3 sts onto cable needle and leave at back of work, K3, then K3 from cable needle; **C6F** = slip next 3 sts onto cable needle and leave at front of work, K3, then K3 from cable needle.

BACK

Using 3¼mm (US 3) needles cast on 122 [136: 152: 168: 190] sts.

Beg and ending rows as indicated and repeating the 8 row patt rep throughout, cont in patt from chart A as folls:

Work 8 rows, ending with RS facing for next row.

Cont in patt, shaping side seams by dec 1 st at each end of next and 3 foll 4th rows. 114 [128: 144: 160: 182] sts.

Work a further 6 rows, ending with **WS** facing for next row.

Row 28 (WS): Patt 0 [0: 4: 8: 19] sts, (M1) 0 [0: 1: 1: 1] times, (patt 4 sts, M1) 0 [0: 0: 1: 1] times, patt 17 [24: 28: 28: 28] sts, M1, patt 4 sts, M1, patt 28 sts, M1, patt 16 sts, M1, patt 28 sts, M1, patt 4 sts, M1, patt 17 [24: 28: 28: 28] sts, (M1, patt 4 sts) 0 [0: 0: 1: 1] times, (M1) 0 [0: 1: 1: 1] times, patt 0 [0: 4: 8: 19] sts. 120 [134: 152: 170: 192] sts.

Change to 3¾mm (US 5) needles.

Beg and ending rows as indicated and repeating the 24 row patt rep throughout, cont in patt from chart B as folls:

Work 2 rows, ending with RS facing for next row.

Inc 1 st at each end of next and every foll 6th row until there are 136 [150: 168: 186: 208] sts, taking inc sts into patt.

Cont straight until back meas 29 [30: 31: 32: 33] cm, ending with RS facing for next row.

Shape armholes

Keeping patt correct, cast off 8 [9: 10: 11: 12] sts at beg of next 2 rows. 120 [132: 148: 164: 184] sts.

Dec 1 st at each end of next 9 [11: 13: 15: 17] rows, then on foll 3 [4: 5: 7: 10] alt rows. 96 [102: 112: 120: 130] sts.

Cont straight until armhole meas 17 [18: 19: 20: 21] cm, ending with RS facing for next row.

Shape shoulders and back neck

Cast off 7 [8: 9: 11: 12] sts at beg of next 2 rows. 82 [86: 94: 98: 106] sts.

Next row (RS): Cast off 7 [8: 9: 11: 12] sts, patt until there are 11 [12: 14: 14: 16] sts on right needle and turn, leaving rem sts on a holder.

Work each side of neck separately.

Cast off 4 sts at beg of next row.

Cast off rem 7 [8: 10: 10: 12] sts.

With RS facing, rejoin yarn to rem sts, cast off centre

46 [46: 48: 48: 50] sts, patt to end.

Complete to match first side, reversing shapings.

LEFT FRONT

Using 3¼mm (US 3) needles cast on 64 [71: 79: 87: 98] sts.

Beg and ending rows as indicated and repeating the 8 row patt rep throughout, cont in patt from chart A as folls:

Row 1 (RS): Work first 61 [68: 76: 84: 95] sts as row 1 of chart A, P1, K2.

Row 2: K1, P1, K1, work last 61 [68: 76: 84: 95] sts as row 2 of chart A.

These 2 rows set the sts.

Cont as set for a further 6 rows, ending with RS facing for next row.

Cont in patt, shaping side seam by dec 1 st at beg of next and 3 foll 4th rows. 60 [67: 75: 83: 94] sts.

Work a further 6 rows, ending with **WS** facing for next row.

Row 28 (WS): Patt 11 sts, M1, patt 28 sts, M1, patt 4 sts, M1, patt 17 [24: 28: 28: 28] sts, (M1, patt 4 sts) 0 [0: 0: 1: 1] times, (M1) 0 [0: 1: 1: 1] times, patt 0 [0: 4: 8: 19] sts. 63 [70: 79: 88: 99] sts.

Change to 3¾mm (US 5) needles.

Beg and ending rows as indicated and repeating the 24 row patt rep throughout, cont in patt from chart B as folls:

Row 1 (RS): Work first 60 [67: 76: 85: 96] sts as row 1 of chart B, K3.

Row 2: K1, P2, work last 60 [67: 76: 85: 96] sts as row 2 of chart B.

These 2 rows set the sts.

Cont as set, inc 1 st at beg of next and every foll 6th row until there are 71 [78: 87: 96: 107] sts, taking inc sts into patt.

Cont straight until 4 rows less have been worked than on back to beg of armhole shaping, ending with RS facing for next row.

Shape front slope

Keeping patt correct, dec 1 st at end of next row and at same edge on foll 3 rows. 67 [74: 83: 92: 103] sts.

Shape armhole

Keeping patt correct, cast off 8 [9: 10: 11: 12] sts at beg and dec 1 st at end of next row. 58 [64: 72: 80: 90] sts.

Dec 1 [1: 1: 1: 0] st at front slope edge of next row. 57 [63: 71: 79: 90] sts.

Dec 1 st at armhole edge of next 9 [11: 13: 15: 17] rows, then on foll 3 [4: 5: 7: 10] alt rows **and at same time** dec 1 st at front slope edge of next

7 [5: 3: 1: 1] rows, then on foll 4 [7: 10: 14: 18] alt rows. 34 [36: 40: 42: 44] sts.
Dec 1 st at front slope edge **only** on 2nd and foll 12 [11: 11: 9: 7] alt rows. 21 [24: 28: 32: 36] sts.
Cont straight until left front matches back to beg of shoulder shaping, ending with RS facing for next row.
Shape shoulder
Cast off 7 [8: 9: 11: 12] sts at beg of next and foll alt row.
Work 1 row.
Cast off rem 7 [8: 10: 10: 12] sts.
Mark positions for 4 buttons along left front opening edge – first to come in row 23, last to come just below beg of front slope shaping, and rem 2 buttons evenly spaced between.

RIGHT FRONT
Using 3¼mm (US 3) needles cast on 64 [71: 79: 87: 98] sts.
Beg and ending rows as indicated and repeating the 8 row patt rep throughout, cont in patt from chart A as folls:
Row 1 (RS): K2, P1, work last 61 [68: 76: 84: 95] sts as row 1 of chart A.
Row 2: Work first 61 [68: 76: 84: 95] sts as row 2 of chart A, K1, P1, K1.
These 2 rows set the sts.
Cont as set for a further 6 rows, ending with RS facing for next row.
Cont in patt, shaping side seam by dec 1 st at end of next and 3 foll 4th rows. 60 [67: 75: 83: 94] sts.
Work 1 row.
Row 23 (buttonhole row) (RS): K1, K2tog, yrn (to make first buttonhole), patt to end.
Working a further 3 buttonholes in this way to correspond with positions marked for buttons and noting that no further reference will be made to buttonholes, cont as folls:
Work a further 4 rows, ending with **WS** facing for next row.
Row 28 (WS): Patt 0 [0: 4: 8: 19] sts, (M1) 0 [0: 1: 1: 1] times, (patt 4 sts, M1) 0 [0: 0: 1: 1] times, patt 17 [24: 28: 28: 28] sts, M1, patt 4 sts, M1, patt 28 sts, M1, patt 11 sts. 63 [70: 79: 88: 99] sts.
Change to 3¼mm (US 5) needles.
Beg and ending rows as indicated and repeating the 24 row patt rep throughout, cont in patt from chart B as folls:
Row 1 (RS): K3, work last 60 [67: 76: 85: 96] sts as row 1 of chart B.

Row 2: Work first 60 [67: 76: 85: 96] sts as row 2 of chart B, P2, K1.
These 2 rows set the sts.
Cont as set, inc 1 st at end of next and every foll 6th row until there are 71 [78: 87: 96: 107] sts, taking inc sts into patt.
Complete to match left front, reversing shapings.

SLEEVES
Using 3¾mm (US 5) needles cast on 108 [112: 116: 120: 124] sts.
Row 1 (RS): P1 [0: 2: 1: 0], (K1, P2) 4 [5: 5: 6: 7] times, ★K8, P2, K8, (P2, K1) 4 times, P2, rep from ★ once more, K8, P2, K8, (P2, K1) 4 [5: 5: 6: 7] times, P1 [0: 2: 1: 0].
Row 2: K1 [0: 2: 1: 0], (P1, K2) 4 [5: 5: 6: 7] times, ★P8, K2, P8, (K2, P1) 4 times, K2, rep from ★ once more, P8, K2, P8, (K2, P1) 4 [5: 5: 6: 7] times, K1 [0: 2: 1: 0].
Row 3: P1 [0: 2: 1: 0], (K1, P2) 4 [5: 5: 6: 7] times, ★C4B, C4F, P2, C4B, C4F, (P2, K1) 4 times, P2, rep from ★ once more, C4B, C4F, P2, C4B, C4F, (P2, K1) 4 [5: 5: 6: 7] times, P1 [0: 2: 1: 0].
Row 4: As row 2.
These 4 rows form patt.
Shape top
Keeping patt correct, cast off 8 [9: 10: 11: 12] sts at beg of next 2 rows. 92 [94: 96: 98: 100] sts.
Dec 1 st at each end of next 3 rows, then on every foll alt row until 82 sts rem, then on foll row, ending with RS facing for next row. 80 sts.
Cast off 3 sts at beg of next 2 rows, 4 sts at beg of foll 2 rows, 6 sts at beg of foll 2 rows, then 8 sts at beg of foll 4 rows.
Cast off rem 22 sts.

MAKING UP
Press as described on the information page.
Join both shoulder seams using back stitch, or mattress stitch if preferred.
Collar
Using 3¼mm (US 3) needles cast on 206 [206: 206: 238: 238] sts.
Row 1 (RS): P2, (K1, P2) 4 times, ★K8, P2, K8, (P2, K1) 4 times, P2, rep from ★ to end.
Row 2: K2, (P1, K2) 4 times, ★P8, K2, P8, (K2, P1) 4 times, K2, rep from ★ to end.

Row 3: P2, (K1, P2) 4 times, ★C4B, C4F, P2, C4B, C4F, (P2, K1) 4 times, P2, rep from ★ to end.

Row 4: As row 2.

These 4 rows form patt.

Keeping patt correct, cast off 4 [4: 4: 5: 5] sts at beg of next 18 [18: 20: 20: 24] rows, then 5 [5: 5: 6: 6] sts at beg of foll 14 [14: 12: 12: 8] rows.

Cast off rem 64 [64: 66: 66: 70] sts in patt.

Matching ends of cast-on edge of collar to beg of front slope shaping, sew row-end and shaped cast-off edges of collar to neck edges.

See information page for finishing instructions, setting in sleeves using the set-in method.

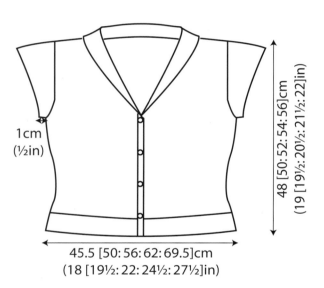

1cm
(½in)

48 [50: 52: 54: 56]cm
(19 [19½: 20½: 21½: 22]in)

45.5 [50: 56: 62: 69.5]cm
(18 [19½: 22: 24½: 27½]in)

key

☐ K on RS, P on WS
⊡ P on RS, K on WS

Cr3R
Cr3L

C6B
C6F

C4B
C4F

Cr 4R
Cr 4L

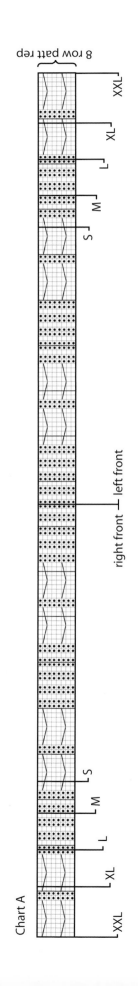

Chart A

8 row patt rep

XXL XL L M S right front ⊥ left front S M L XL XXL

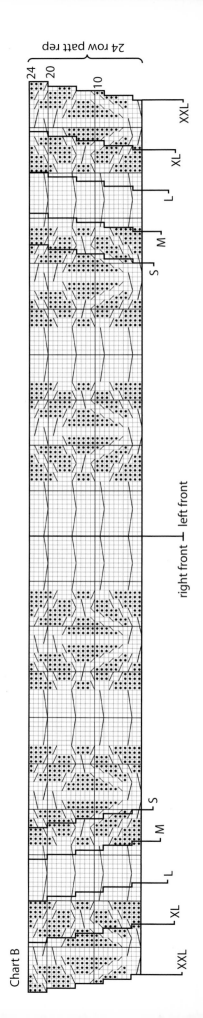

Chart B

24 row patt rep

24 20 10

XXL XL L M S right front ⊥ left front S M L XL XXL

YARN

	8	10	12	14	16	18	
To fit bust	81	86	91	97	102	107	cm
	32	34	36	38	40	42	in

Rowan Milk Cotton DK

A Liquorice 099	2	2	2	2	2	2	x	50gm
B Scented Satin 088	2	2	2	2	2	2	x	50gm
C Aniseed 090	2	2	2	2	2	2	x	50gm
D Water Bomb 098	2	2	2	2	2	2	x	50gm
E Midget Gem 097	1	1	1	1	1	1	x	50gm

NEEDLES

1 pair 3¼mm (no 10) (US 3) needles
1 pair 3¾mm (no 9) (US 5) needles
3¼mm (no 10) (US 3) circular needle

BUTTONS – 6 x BN1028

TENSION

24 sts and 26 rows to 10 cm measured over patterned st st using 3¾mm (US 5) needles.

Gerty

BACK

Using 3¾mm (US 5) needles and yarn A cast on 95 [99: 105: 111: 119: 127] sts.
Beg and ending rows as indicated, using the **fairisle** technique as described on the information page, beg with chart row 21 and repeating the 12 row patt repeat throughout, now work in patt from chart, which is worked entirely in st st beg with a K row, as folls:
Dec 1 st at each end of 3rd and foll 4th row.
91 [95: 101: 107: 115: 123] sts.
Work 7 rows, ending with RS facing for next row.
Inc 1 st at each end of next and every foll 8th row until there are 101 [105: 111: 117: 125: 133] sts, taking inc sts into patt.
Cont straight until back meas 23 [23: 22: 24: 23: 23] cm, ending with RS facing for next row.
Shape armholes
Keeping patt correct, cast off 6 [7: 7: 8: 8: 9] sts at beg of next 2 rows.
89 [91: 97: 101: 109: 115] sts.
Dec 1 st at each end of next 7 [7: 9: 9: 11: 11] rows, then on foll 6 [6: 6: 6: 6: 7] alt rows. 63 [65: 67: 71: 75: 79] sts.
Cont straight until armhole meas 18 [18: 19: 19: 20: 20] cm, ending with RS facing for next row.
Shape shoulders and back neck
Next row (RS): Cast off 5 [5: 6: 7: 7: 8] sts, K until there are 8 [9: 9: 10: 11: 12] sts on right needle and turn, leaving rem sts on a holder.
Work each side of neck separately.
Cast off 3 sts at beg of next row.
Cast off rem 5 [6: 6: 7: 8: 9] sts.
With RS facing, rejoin yarns to rem sts, cast off centre 37 [37: 37: 37: 39: 39] sts, K to end.
Complete to match first side, reversing shapings.

LEFT FRONT

Using 3¾mm (US 5) needles and yarn C cast on 3 sts.
Beg and ending rows as indicated and beg with chart row 1, now work in patt from chart as folls:
Work 1 row.
Inc 1 st at each end of next 18 rows, taking inc sts into patt and ending with **WS** facing for next row. 39 sts.
Cast on 4 sts at beg and inc 1 st at end of next row, then cast on 2 [4: 7:

10: 14: 18] sts at beg of foll row.
46 [48: 51: 54: 58: 62] sts.
Work 1 row, ending with RS facing for next row.
Dec 1 st at beg of next and foll 4th row.
44 [46: 49: 52: 56: 60] sts.
Work 7 rows, ending with RS facing for next row.
Inc 1 st at beg of next and every foll 8th row until there are 49 [51: 54: 57: 61: 65] sts, taking inc sts into patt.
Cont straight until 5 rows less have been worked than on back to beg of armhole shaping, ending with **WS** facing for next row.
Shape neck
Keeping patt correct, cast off 6 [6: 6: 6: 7: 7] sts at beg of next row.
43 [45: 48: 51: 54: 58] sts.
Dec 1 st at neck edge of next 4 rows, ending with RS facing for next row.
39 [41: 44: 47: 50: 54] sts.
Shape armhole
Keeping patt correct, cast off 6 [7: 7: 8: 8: 9] sts at beg and dec 1 st at end of next row. 32 [33: 36: 38: 41: 44] sts.
Work 1 row.
Dec 1 st at neck edge of next and foll 4 alt rows, then on 3 foll 4th rows, then on foll 6th row **and at same time**
dec 1 st at armhole edge of next 7 [7: 9: 9: 11: 11] rows,
then on foll 6 [6: 6: 6: 6: 7] alt rows. 10 [11: 12: 14: 15: 17] sts.
Cont straight until left front matches back to beg of shoulder shaping, ending with RS facing for next row.
Shape shoulder
Cast off 5 [5: 6: 7: 7: 8] sts at beg of next row.
Work 1 row.
Cast off rem 5 [6: 6: 7: 8: 9] sts.

RIGHT FRONT

Using 3¾mm (US 5) needles and yarn C cast on 3 sts.
Beg and ending rows as indicated and beg with chart row 1, now work in patt from chart as folls:
Work 1 row.
Inc 1 st at each end of next 18 rows, taking inc sts into patt and ending with **WS** facing for next row. 39 sts.
Cast on 3 [5: 8: 11: 15: 19] sts at beg and inc 1 st at end of next row, then

cast on 3 sts at beg of foll row.
46 [48: 51: 54: 58: 62] sts.
Work 1 row, ending with RS facing for next row.
Dec 1 st at end of next and foll 4th row.
44 [46: 49: 52: 56: 60] sts.
Complete to match left front, reversing shapings.

MAKING UP

Press as described on the information page.
Join both shoulder seams using back stitch, or mattress stitch if preferred.

Neckband

With RS facing, using 3¼mm (US 3) needles and yarn A, beg and ending at front opening edges, pick up and knit 62 [62: 64: 64: 67: 67] sts up right side of neck, 44 [44: 44: 44: 46: 46] sts from back, then 62 [62: 64: 64: 67: 67] sts down left side of neck. 168 [168: 172: 172: 180: 180] sts.
Row 1 (WS): K1, P2, *K2, P2, rep from * to last st, K1.
Row 2: K3, *P2, K2, rep from * to last st, K1.
These 2 rows form rib.
Work in rib for a further 3 rows, ending with RS facing for next row.
Cast off in rib.

Armhole borders (both alike)

With RS facing, using 3¼mm (US 3) needles and yarn A, pick up and knit 102 [102: 106: 110: 114: 114] sts evenly all round armhole edge.
Row 1 (WS): P2, *K2, P2, rep from * to end.
Row 2: K2, *P2, K2, rep from * to end.
These 2 rows form rib.
Work in rib for a further 3 rows, ending with RS facing for next row.
Cast off in rib.
Join side and armhole border seams.

Hem border

With RS facing, using 3¼mm (US 3) circular needle and yarn A, beg and ending at front opening edges, pick up and knit 25 sts down first side of left front point, 3 sts from cast-on edge of left front point (place marker on centre st of these 3 sts), 26 [28: 31: 34: 38: 42] sts up other side of left front point to base of side seam, 94 [98: 104: 110: 118: 126] sts from cast-on edge of back, 26 [28: 31: 34: 38: 42] sts down first side of right front point, 3 sts from cast-on edge of right front point (place marker on centre st of these 3 sts), then 25 sts up other side of right front point to base of front opening edge.

202 [210: 222: 234: 250: 266] sts.
Row 1 (WS): K1, (P2, K2) 6 times, P3 (marked st is centre st of these 3 sts), K2, *P2, K2, rep from * to last 28 sts, P3 (marked st is centre st of these 3 sts), (K2, P2) 6 times, K1.
This row sets position of rib as given for neckband.
Keeping rib correct and taking inc sts into rib, cont as folls:
Row 2: *Rib to marked st, M1, K marked st, M1, rep from * once more, rib to end.
Row 3: *Rib to marked st, M1, P marked st, M1, rep from * once more, rib to end.
Rep last 2 rows once more. 218 [226: 238: 250: 266: 282] sts.
Cast off in rib.

Button band

With RS facing, using 3¼mm (US 3) needles and yarn A, pick up and knit 60 sts evenly down left front opening edge, from cast-off edge of neckband to cast-off edge of hem border.
Beg with row 1, work in rib as given for neckband for 5 rows, ending with RS facing for next row.
Cast off in rib.

Buttonhole band

With RS facing, using 3¼mm (US 3) needles and yarn A, pick up and knit 60 sts evenly up right front opening edge, from cast-off edge of hem border to cast-off edge of neckband.
Beg with row 1, work in rib as given for neckband for 1 row, ending with RS facing for next row.
Row 2 (RS): Rib 2, *work 2 tog, yrn (to make a buttonhole), rib 16, rep from * twice more, work 2 tog, yrn (to make 4th buttonhole), rib 2.
Work in rib for a further 3 rows, ending with RS facing for next row.
Cast off in rib.

Pocket trims (make 2)

Using 3¼mm (US 3) needles and yarn A cast on 28 sts.
Beg with row 2, work in rib as given for neckband for 5 rows, ending with **WS** facing for next row.
Cast off in rib (on **WS**).
Using photograph as a guide, sew pocket trims onto fronts, attaching a button centrally onto each trim.
See information page for finishing instructions.

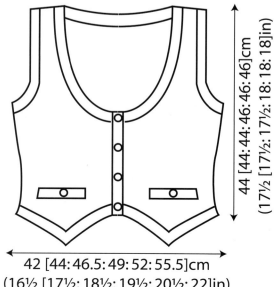

44 [44: 44: 46: 46: 46]cm
(17½ [17½: 17½: 18: 18: 18]in)

42 [44: 46.5: 49: 52: 55.5]cm
(16½ [17½: 18½: 19½: 20½: 22]in)

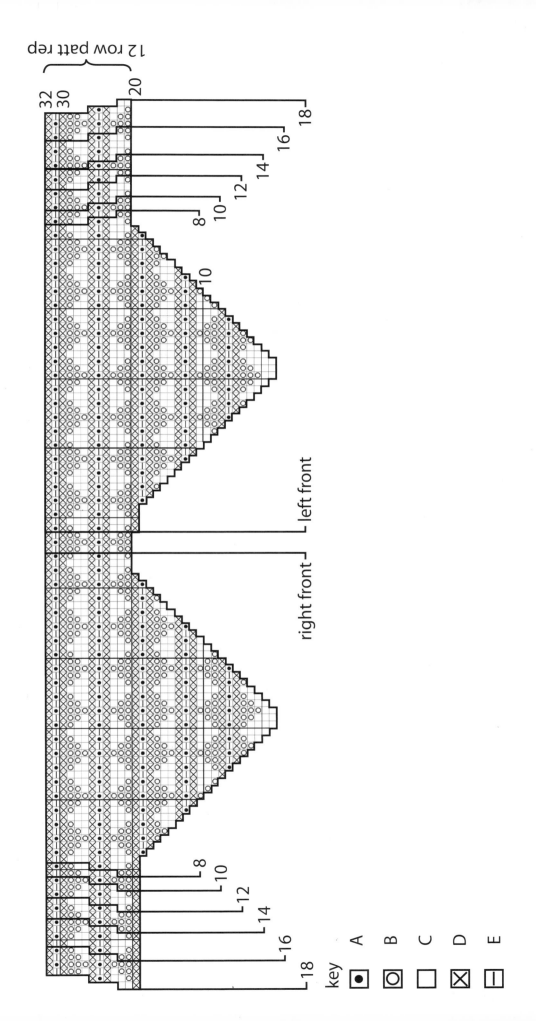

12 row patt rep

32
30
20

18
16
14
12
10
8

10

left front

right front

8
10
12
14
16
18

key
A ●
B ○
C ☐
D ☒
E ⊟

Camellia

YARN

	S	M	L	XL	XXL	
To fit bust	81-86	91-97	102-107	112-117	122-127	cm
	32-34	36-38	40-42	44-46	48-50	in

Rowan Fine Milk Cotton
A Water Bomb 498

	6	7	8	9	9	x	50gm

B Tutti Frutti 487

	1	1	1	1	1	x	50gm

NEEDLES
1 pair 2¼mm (no 13) (US 1) needles

EXTRAS – approx 2.00 [2.50: 3.00: 3.50: 4.00] m of 6mm wide elastic and matching sewing thread

TENSION
30 sts and 40 rows to 10 cm measured over patt using 2¼mm (US 1) needles.

Pattern note: When working lace patt from chart, ensure that a dec is worked for every inc (yfwd) so that number of sts remains constant (except where shaping occurs). You may find it helpful to place markers between each 20 st patt rep and, when working shaping, work sts beyond markers in st st.

BACK
Using 2¼mm (US 1) needles and yarn B cast on 144 [160: 178: 196: 216] sts.
Break off yarn B and join in yarn A.
Beg with a K row, work in st st for 24 rows, ending with RS facing for next row.
Beg and ending rows as indicated and repeating the 44 row patt repeat throughout, now work in patt from chart as folls:
Cont straight until back meas 26 [27: 28: 29: 30] cm, ending with RS facing for next row.
Shape armholes
Keeping patt correct, cast off 8 [9: 10: 11: 12] sts at beg of next 2 rows.
128 [142: 158: 174: 192] sts.★★
Dec 1 st at each end of next 9 [11: 13: 15: 17] rows, then on foll 7 [9: 10: 12: 14] alt rows. 96 [102: 112: 120: 130] sts.
Cont straight until armhole meas 18 [19: 20: 21: 22] cm, ending with RS facing for next row.
Shape shoulders and back neck
Cast off 6 [7: 8: 10: 11] sts at beg of next 2 rows.
84 [88: 96: 100: 108] sts.
Next row (RS): Cast off 6 [7: 8: 10: 11] sts, patt until there are 10 [11: 13: 13: 15] sts on right needle and turn, leaving rem sts on a holder.
Work each side of neck separately.
Cast off 4 sts at beg of next row.
Cast off rem 6 [7: 9: 9: 11] sts.
With RS facing, rejoin yarn to rem sts, cast off centre 52 [52: 54: 54: 56] sts, patt to end.
Complete to match first side, reversing shapings.

FRONT
Work as given for back to ★★.
Dec 1 st at each end of next 9 [11: 13: 15: 17] rows, then on foll 6 [5: 4: 3: 2] alt rows. 98 [110: 124: 138: 154] sts.
Work 1 row, ending with RS facing for next row.
Shape neck
Next row (RS): Work 2 tog, patt 36 [42: 48: 55: 62] sts and turn, leaving rem sts on a holder.
Work each side of neck separately.
Keeping patt correct, cast off 5 sts at beg of next row.

32 [38: 44: 51: 58] sts.
Dec 1 st at neck edge of next 7 rows, then on foll 5 alt rows, then on 2 foll 4th rows **and at same time** dec 1 st at armhole edge of 0 [next: next: next: next] and foll 0 [2: 4: 7: 10] alt rows. 18 [21: 25: 29: 33] sts.
Cont straight until front matches back to beg of shoulder shaping, ending with RS facing for next row.
Shape shoulder
Cast off 6 [7: 8: 10: 11] sts at beg of next and foll alt row.
Work 1 row.
Cast off rem 6 [7: 9: 9: 11] sts.
With RS facing, rejoin yarn to rem sts, cast off centre 22 [22: 24: 24: 26] sts, patt to last 2 sts, work 2 tog.
Complete to match first side, reversing shapings.

SLEEVES
Using 2¼mm (US 1) needles and yarn B cast on 108 [112: 116: 120: 124] sts.
Break off yarn B and join in yarn A.
Beg with a K row, work in st st until sleeve meas 12 cm, ending with RS facing for next row.
Shape top
Cast off 8 [9: 10: 11: 12] sts at beg of next 2 rows.
92 [94: 96: 98: 100] sts.
Dec 1 st at each end of next 5 rows, then on every foll alt row until 64 sts rem, then on foll 11 rows, ending with RS facing for next row. 42 sts.
Cast off 5 sts at beg of next 4 rows.
Cast off rem 22 sts.

MAKING UP
Press as described on the information page.
Join right shoulder seam using back stitch, or mattress stitch if preferred.
Neckband
With RS facing, using 2¼mm (US 1) needles and yarn B, pick up and knit 42 [45: 48: 51: 54] sts down left side of neck, 22 [22: 24: 24: 26] sts from front, 42 [45: 48: 51: 54] sts up right side of neck, then 60 [60: 62: 62: 64] sts from back. 166 [172: 182: 188: 198] sts.
Cast off knitwise (on **WS**).
See information page for finishing instructions, setting in sleeves using the set-in method.

From elastic, cut 2 lengths that fit snugly around waist when slightly stretched. Join ends of each length to form 2 loops.

Place first loop against WS of body 2 cm up from cast-on edge and machine stitch in place, stretching elastic as you sew.

Attach 2nd loop in same way, positioning this loop 1.5 cm above first loop. In same way, cut 2 lengths of elastic that fit snugly around top of arm when slightly stretched. Join ends to form 2 loops. Place each loop against WS of each sleeve 2.5 cm up from cast-on edge and machine stitch in place, stretching elastic as you sew.

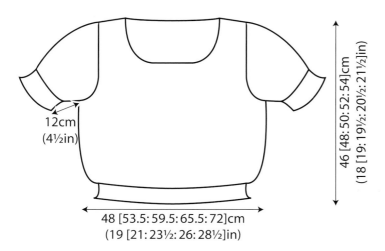

12cm
(4½in)

48 [53.5: 59.5: 65.5: 72]cm
(19 [21: 23½: 26: 28½]in)

46 [48: 50: 52: 54]cm
(18 [19: 19½: 20½: 21½]in)

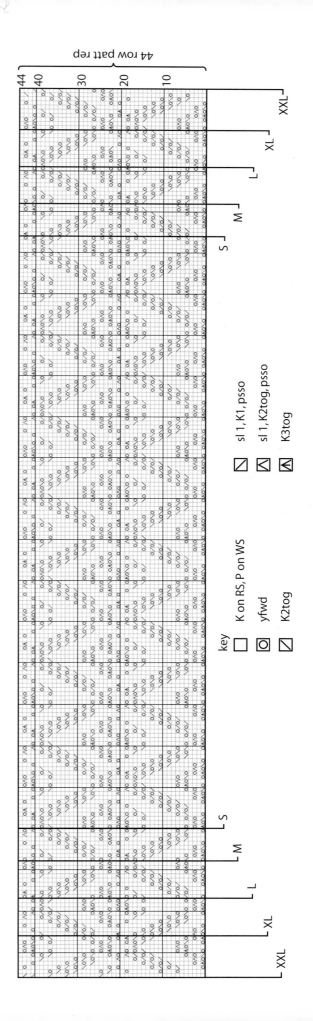

44 row patt rep

key

☐ K on RS, P on WS	☑ sl 1, K1, psso
⊙ yfwd	◩ sl 1, K2tog, psso
◪ K2tog	◣ K3tog

Harmonie ••

YARN

			S	M	L	XL	XXL		
To fit bust			81-86	91-97	102-107	112-117	122-127		cm
			32-34	36-38	40-42	44-46	48-50		in
Rowan Milk Cotton DK									
A	Water Bomb	098	2	3	3	3	3	x	50gm
B	Liquorice	099	2	2	2	2	2	x	50gm
C	Tutti Frutti	087	2	2	2	2	2	x	50gm
D	Aniseed	090	2	2	2	2	2	x	50gm
E	Jelly Baby	096	2	2	2	2	2	x	50gm
F	Midget Gem	097	2	2	2	2	2	x	50gm
G	Barley Sugar	081	2	2	2	2	2	x	50gm
H	Scented Satin	088	2	2	2	2	2	x	50gm

NEEDLES

1 pair 3¼mm (no 10) (US 3) needles & 1 pair 3¾mm (no 9) (US 5) needles

TENSION

26 sts and 50 rows to 10 cm measured over patt using 3¾mm (US 5) needles

Pattern note: When working patt, work all slipped sts with yarn held at **WS** of work – at back on RS rows, and at front on WS rows.

STRIPE SEQUENCE
Rows 1 and 2: Using yarn B.
Rows 3 and 4: Using yarn C.
Rows 5 and 6: Using yarn D.
Rows 7 and 8: Using yarn E.
Rows 9 and 10: Using yarn F.
Rows 11 and 12: Using yarn G.
Rows 13 and 14: Using yarn H.
Rows 15 and 16: Using yarn A.
These 16 rows form stripe sequence and are repeated.

BACK
Using 3¼mm (US 3) needles and yarn A cast on 109 [119: 129: 143: 159] sts.
Row 1 (RS): K1, ★P1, K1, rep from ★ to end.
Row 2: As row 1.
These 2 rows form moss st.
Cont in moss st for a further 5 rows, ending with **WS** facing for next row.
Row 8 (WS): P5 [4: 4: 6: 2], M1, (P5, M1, P6 [6: 6: 5: 6], M1) 9 [10: 11: 13: 14] times, P5 [5: 4: 7: 3]. 128 [140: 152: 170: 188] sts.
Change to 3¾mm (US 5) needles.
Joining in colours as required, cont in patt as folls:
Row 1 (RS): Using yarn B, K1, ★sl 2, K4, rep from ★ to last st, K1.
Row 2: Using yarn B, P1, ★K2, P2, sl 2, rep from ★ to last st, P1.
Row 3: Using yarn C, K3, sl 2, ★K4, sl 2, rep from ★ to last 3 sts, K3.
Row 4: Using yarn C, P3, sl 2, K2, ★P2, sl 2, K2, rep from ★ to last st, P1.
Row 5: Using yarn D, K5, sl 2, ★K4, sl 2, rep from ★ to last st, K1.
Row 6: Using yarn D, P1, ★sl 2, K2, P2, rep from ★ to last st, P1.
These 6 rows form patt and place first 6 rows of stripe sequence.
Beg with stripe sequence row 7, cont in 16 row stripe sequence **and** 6 row patt rep, shaping side seams by dec 1 st at each end of 5th and every foll 8th row until 118 [130: 142: 160: 178] sts rem.
Work 21 rows, ending with RS facing for next row.
Inc 1 st at each end of next and every foll 14th row until there are 128 [140: 152: 170: 188] sts, taking inc sts into patt.
Cont straight until back meas 32 [33: 34: 35: 36] cm, ending with RS facing for next row.

Shape armholes
Keeping patt correct, cast off 6 [7: 8: 9: 10] sts at beg of next 2 rows.

116 [126: 136: 152: 168] sts.
Dec 1 st at each end of next 7 [9: 11: 13: 15] rows, then on foll 4 [5: 4: 6: 7] alt rows. 94 [98: 106: 114: 124] sts.
Cont straight until armhole meas 19 [20: 21: 22: 23] cm, ending with RS facing for next row.
Shape shoulders and back neck
Next row (RS): Cast off 6 [7: 8: 9: 10] sts, patt until there are 15 [16: 18: 21: 24] sts on right needle and turn, leaving rem sts on a holder.
Work each side of neck separately.
Dec 1 st at neck edge of next 3 rows **and at same time** cast off 6 [7: 8: 9: 10] sts at beg of 2nd row.
Cast off rem 6 [6: 7: 9: 11] sts.
With RS facing, rejoin appropriate yarn to rem sts, cast off centre 52 [52: 54: 54: 56] sts, patt to end.
Complete to match first side, reversing shapings.

FRONT
Work as given for back to beg of armhole shaping.
Shape armholes and divide for neck
Next row (RS): Cast off 6 [7: 8: 9: 10] sts, patt until there are 56 [61: 66: 74: 82] sts on right needle after cast-off and turn, leaving rem sts on a holder.
Work each side of neck separately.
Work 1 row.
Keeping patt correct, dec 1 st at armhole edge of next 7 [9: 11: 13: 15] rows, then on foll 4 [5: 4: 6: 7] alt rows **and at same time** dec 1 st at neck edge of next and foll 7 [9: 9: 8: 7] alt rows, then on 0 [0: 0: 2: 3] foll 4th rows. 37 [37: 41: 44: 49] sts.
Dec 1 st at neck edge **only** on 2nd [2nd: 2nd: 4th: 2nd] and foll 5 [1: 0: 0: 0] alt rows, then on 13 [15: 17: 16: 17] foll 4th rows. 18 [20: 23: 27: 31] sts.
Cont straight until front matches back to beg of shoulder shaping, ending with RS facing for next row.
Shape shoulder
Cast off 6 [7: 8: 9: 10] sts at beg of next and foll alt row.
Work 1 row.

Cast off rem 6 [6: 7: 9: 11] sts.
With RS facing, rejoin appropriate yarn to rem sts, cast off centre 4 sts, patt to end.
Complete to match first side, reversing shapings.

SLEEVES

Using 3¼mm (US 3) needles and yarn A cast on 63 [63: 67: 67: 73] sts.
Work in moss st as given for back for 7 rows, ending with **WS** facing for next row.

Row 8 (WS): P4 [4: 3: 3: 3], M1, (P5, M1, P6 [6: 5: 5: 6], M1) 5 [5: 6: 6: 6] times, P4. 74 [74: 80: 80: 86] sts.

Change to 3¾mm (US 5) needles.

Joining in colours as required, cont in patt as given for back, shaping sides by inc 1 st at each end of 3rd and foll 5 [9: 7: 11: 9] alt rows, then on 4 [2: 3: 1: 2] foll 4th rows, taking inc sts into patt.
94 [98: 102: 106: 110] sts.

Cont straight until sleeve meas 10 cm, ending with RS facing for next row.

Shape top

Keeping patt correct, cast off 6 [7: 8: 9: 10] sts at beg of next 2 rows.
82 [84: 86: 88: 90] sts.

Dec 1 st at each end of next 3 rows, then on foll 10 alt rows, then on every foll 4th row until 46 sts rem.

Work 1 row.

Dec 1 st at each end of next and foll 8 alt rows, then on foll 5 rows, ending with RS facing for next row. 18 sts.

Cast off 3 sts at beg of next 2 rows.

Cast off rem 12 sts.

MAKING UP

Press as described on the information page.

Join both shoulder seams using back stitch, or mattress stitch if preferred.

Neckband and ties

Using 3¼mm (US 3) needles and yarn A cast on 5 sts.

Work in moss st as given for back for 28 cm, ending with RS facing for next row. (This section forms first tie end.)

Place marker at beg of last row. (This marker matches to one end of 4 cast-off sts at base of front neck.)

Cont in moss st until strip, from marker and when slightly stretched, fits up right front slope, across back neck and down left front slope, beg and ending at either side of 4 cast-off sts at base of front neck and ending with RS facing for next row. (This section forms neckband.)

Place marker at beg of last row. (This marker matches to other end of 4 cast-off sts at base of front neck.)

Cont in moss st for a further 28 cm from second marker, ending with RS facing for next row. (This section forms second tie end.)

Cast off in moss st.

See information page for finishing instructions, setting in sleeves using the set-in method.

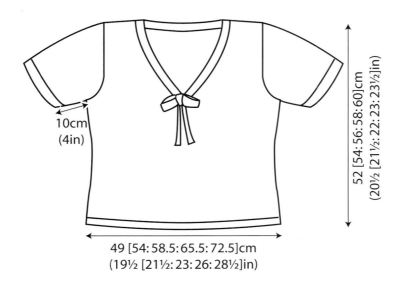

10cm
(4in)

49 [54: 58.5: 65.5: 72.5]cm
(19½ [21½: 23: 26: 28½]in)

52 [54: 56: 58: 60]cm
(20½ [21½: 22: 23: 23½]in)

information

TENSION

Obtaining the correct tension is perhaps the single factor which can make the difference between a successful garment and a disastrous one. It controls both the shape and size of an article, so any variation, however slight, can distort the finished garment. Different designers feature in our books and it is their tension, given at the start of each pattern, which you must match. We recommend that you knit a square in pattern and/or stocking stitch (depending on the pattern instructions) of perhaps 5 - 10 more stitches and 5 - 10 more rows than those given in the tension note. Mark out the central 10cm square with pins. If you have too many stitches to 10cm try again using thicker needles, if you have too few stitches to 10cm try again using finer needles. Once you have achieved the correct tension your garment will be knitted to the measurements indicated in the size diagram shown at the end of the pattern.

SIZING & SIZE DIAGRAM NOTE

The instructions are given for the smallest size. Where they vary, work the figures in brackets for the larger sizes. One set of figures refers to all sizes. Included with most patterns in this magazine is a 'size diagram', or sketch of the finished garment and its dimensions. To help you choose the size of garment to knit please refer to the NEW sizing guide on page 102.

KNITTING WITH COLOUR

There are two main methods of working colour into a knitted fabric: Intarsia and Fairisle techniques. The first method produces a single thickness of fabric and is usually used where a colour is only required in a particular area of a row and does not form a repeating pattern across the row, as in the fairisle technique.

Intarsia: The simplest way to do this is to cut short lengths of yarn for each motif or block of colour used in a row. Then joining in the various colours at the appropriate point on the row, link one colour to the next by twisting them around each other where they meet on the wrong side to avoid gaps. All ends can then either be darned along the colour join lines, as each motif is completed or then can be " knitted-in" to the fabric of the knitting as each colour is worked into the pattern. This is done in much the same way as "weaving- in" yarns when working the Fairisle technique and does save time darning-in ends. It is essential that the tension is noted for Intarsia as this may vary from the stocking stitch if both are used in the same pattern.

Fair isle type knitting: When two or three colours are worked repeatedly across a row, strand the yarn not in use loosely behind the stitches being worked. If you are working with more than two colours, treat the "floating" yarns as if they were one yarn and always spread the stitches to their correct width to keep them elastic. It is advisable not to carry the stranded or "floating" yarns over more than three stitches at a time, but to weave them under and over the colour you are working.

The "floating" yarns are therefore caught at the back of the work.

FINISHING INSTRUCTIONS

After working for hours knitting a garment, it seems a great pity that many garments are spoiled because such little care is taken in the pressing and finishing process. Follow the following tips for a truly professional-looking garment.

PRESSING

Block out each piece of knitting and following the instructions on the ball band press the garment pieces, omitting the ribs. Tip: Take special care to press the edges, as this will make sewing up both easier and neater. If the ball band indicates that the fabric is not to be pressed, then covering the blocked out fabric with a damp white cotton cloth and leaving it to stand will have the desired effect. Darn in all ends neatly along the selvage edge or a colour join, as appropriate.

STITCHING

When stitching the pieces together, remember to match areas of colour and texture very carefully where they meet. Use a seam stitch such as back stitch or mattress stitch for all main knitting seams and join all ribs and neckband with mattress stitch, unless otherwise stated.

CONSTRUCTION

Having completed the pattern instructions, join left shoulder and neckband seams as detailed above. Sew the top of the sleeve to the body of the garment using the method detailed in the pattern, referring to the appropriate guide:

Straight cast-off sleeves: Place centre of cast-off edge of sleeve to shoulder seam. Sew top of sleeve to body, using markers as guidelines where applicable.

Square set-in sleeves: Place centre of cast-off edge of sleeve to shoulder seam. Set sleeve head into armhole, the straight sides at top of sleeve to form a neat right-angle to cast-off sts at armhole on back and front.

Shallow set-in sleeves: Place centre of cast off edge of sleeve to shoulder seam. Match decreases at beg of armhole shaping to decreases at top of sleeve. Sew sleeve head into armhole, easing in shapings.

Set- in sleeves: Place centre of cast-off edge of sleeve to shoulder seam. Set in sleeve, easing sleeve head into armhole.

Join side and sleeve seams.
Slip stitch pocket edgings and linings into place.
Sew on buttons to correspond with buttonholes.
Ribbed welts and neckbands and any areas of garter stitch should not be pressed.

CHART NOTE

Many of the patterns in the book are worked from charts. Each square on a chart represents a stitch and each line of squares a row of knitting. Each colour used is given a different letter and these are shown in the materials section, or in the key alongside the chart of each pattern. When working from the charts, read odd rows (K) from right to left and even rows (P) from left to right, unless otherwise stated. When working lace from a chart it is important to note that all but the largest size may have to alter the first and last few stitches in order not to lose or gain stitches over the row.

WORKING A LACE PATTERN

When working a lace pattern it is important to remember that if you are unable to work both the increase and corresponding decrease and vica versa, the stitches should be worked in stocking stitch.

K	knit
P	purl
st(s)	stitch(es)
inc	increas(e)(ing)
dec	decreas(e)(ing)
st st	stocking stitch (1 row K, 1 row P)
g st	garter stitch (K every row)
beg	begin(ning)
foll	following
rem	remain(ing)
rev st st	reverse stocking stitch (1 row K , 1 row P)
rep	repeat
alt	alternate
cont	continue
patt	pattern
tog	together

mm	millimetres
cm	centimetres
in(s)	inch(es)
RS	right side
WS	wrong side
sl 1	slip one stitch
psso	pass slipped stitch over
p2sso	pass 2 slipped stitches over
tbl	through back of loop
M1	make one stitch by picking up horizontal loop before next stitch and knitting into back of it
M1P	make one stitch by picking up horizontal loop before next stitch and purling into back of it
yfwd	yarn forward
yrn	yarn round needle
meas	measures

0	no stitches, times or rows
-	no stitches, times or rows for that size
yo	yarn over needle
yfrn	yarn forward round needle
wyib	with yarn at back
sl 2	slip 2 stitches

Crochet Terms

UK crochet terms and abbreviations have been used throughout. The list below gives the US equivalent where they vary.

ABBREV.	UK	US
dc	double crochet	single crochet
htr	half treble	half double crochet
tr	treble	double crochet

• Easy, straight forward knitting   •• Suitable for the average knitter   ••• For the more experienced knitter

sizing guide

Our sizing now conforms to standard clothing sizes. Therefore if you buy a standard size 12 in clothing, then our size 12 or Medium patterns will fit you perfectly.

Dimensions in the charts shown are body measurements, not garment dimensions, therefore please refer to the measuring guide to help you to determine which is the best size for you to knit.

CASUAL SIZING GUIDE FOR WOMEN

As there are some designs that are intended to fit more generously, we have introduced our casual sizing guide. The designs that fall into this group can be recognised by the size range: Small, Medium, Large & Xlarge. Each of these sizes cover two sizes from the standard sizing guide, ie. Size S will fit sizes 8/10, size M will fit sizes 12/14 and so on. The sizing within this chart is also based on the larger size within the range, ie. M will be based on size 14.

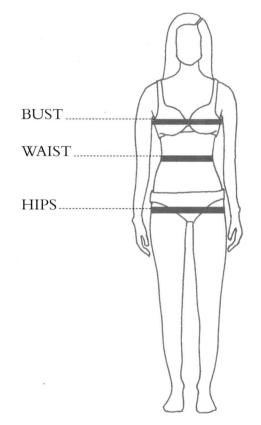

BUST

WAIST

HIPS

UK SIZE DUAL SIZE	S 8/10	M 12/14	L 16/18	XL 20/22	XXL 24/26	
To fit bust	32 – 34	36 – 38	40 – 42	44 – 46	48 - 50	inches
	82 – 87	92 - 97	102 – 107	112 – 117	122 - 127	cm
To fit waist	24 – 26	28 – 30	32 – 34	36 – 38	40 - 50	inches
	61 – 66	71 – 76	81 – 86	91 – 96	101 - 106	cm
To fit hips	34 – 36	38 – 40	42 – 44	46 – 48	50 - 52	inches
	87 – 92	97 – 102	107 – 112	117 – 122	127 - 132	cm

STANDARD SIZING GUIDE FOR WOMEN

UK SIZE	8	10	12	14	16	18	20	22	
USA Size	6	8	10	12	14	16	18	20	
EUR Size	34	36	38	40	42	44	46	48	
To fit bust	32	34	36	38	40	42	44	46	inches
	82	87	92	97	102	107	112	117	cm
To fit waist	24	26	28	30	32	34	36	38	inches
	61	66	71	76	81	86	91	96	cm
To fit hips	34	6	38	40	42	44	46	48	inches
	87	92	97	102	107	112	117	122	cm

MEASURING GUIDE

For maximum comfort and to ensure the correct fit when choosing a size to knit, please follow the tips below when checking your size. Measure yourself close to your body, over your underwear and don't pull the tape measure too tight!

Bust/chest – measure around the fullest part of the bust/chest and across the shoulder blades.

Waist – measure around the natural waistline, just above the hip bone.

Hips – measure around the fullest part of the bottom.

If you don't wish to measure yourself, note the size of a favourite jumper that you like the fit of. Our sizes are now comparable to the clothing sizes from the major high street retailers, so if your favourite jumper is a size Medium or size 12, then our casual size Medium and standard size 12 should be approximately the same fit.

To be extra sure, measure your favourite jumper and then compare these measurements with the Rowan size diagram given at the end of the individual instructions.

Finally, once you have decided which size is best for you, please ensure that you achieve the tension required for the design you wish to knit.

Remember if your tension is too loose, your garment will be bigger than the pattern size and you may use more yarn. If your tension is too tight, your garment could be smaller than the pattern size and you will have yarn left over.

Furthermore if your tension is incorrect, the handle of your fabric will be too stiff or floppy and will not fit properly. It really does make sense to check your tension before starting every project.

AUSTRALIA: Australian Country Spinners, Pty Ltd, Level 7, 409 St. Kilda Road, Melbourne Vic 3004. Tel: 03 9380 3830 Fax: 03 9820 0989 Email: sales@auspinners.com.au

AUSTRIA: Coats Harlander GmbH, Autokaderstrasse 31, A -1210 Wien. Tel: (01) 27716 – 0   Fax: (01) 27716 - 228

BELGIUM: Coats Benelux, Ring Oost 14A, Ninove, 9400, Belgium Tel: 0346 35 37 00 Email: sales.coatsninove@coats.com

CANADA: Westminster Fibers Inc, 165 Ledge St, Nashua, NH03060 Tel: (1 603) 886 5041 / 5043   Fax: (1 603) 886 1056 Email: rowan@westminsterfibers.com

CHINA: Coats Shanghai Ltd, No 9 Building , Baosheng Road, Songjiang Industrial Zone, Shanghai. Tel: (86- 21) 5774 3733   Fax: (86-21) 5774 3768

DENMARK: Coats Danmark A/S, Nannasgade 28, 2200 Kobenhavn N Tel: (45) 35 86 90 50   Fax: (45) 35 82 15 10 Email: info@hpgruppen.dk Web: www.hpgruppen.dk

FINLAND: Coats Opti Oy, Ketjutie 3, 04220 Kerava Tel: (358) 9 274 871   Fax: (358) 9 2748 7330 Email: coatsopti.sales@coats.com

FRANCE: Coats France / Steiner Frères, SAS 100, avenue du Général de Gaulle, 18 500 Mehun-Sur-Yèvre Tel: (33) 02 48 23 12 30   Fax: (33) 02 48 23 12 40

GERMANY: Coats GMbH, Kaiserstrasse 1, D-79341 Kenzingen Tel: (49) 7644 8020   Fax: (49) 7644 802399 Web: www.coatsgmbh.de

HOLLAND: Coats Benelux, Ring Oost 14A, Ninove, 9400, Belgium Tel: 0346 35 37 00 Email: sales.coatsninove@coats.com

HONG KONG: Coats China Holdings Ltd, 19/F Millennium City 2, 378 Kwun Tong Road, Kwun Tong, Kowloon Tel: (852) 2798 6886   Fax: (852) 2305 0311

ICELAND: Storkurinn, Laugavegi 59, 101 Reykjavik Tel: (354) 551 8258 Email: storkurinn@simnet.is

ITALY: Coats Cucirini s.r.l., Via Sarca 223, 20126 Milano Tel: 800 992377   Fax: 0266111701 Email: servizio.clienti@coats.com

KOREA: Coats Korea Co Ltd, 5F Kuckdong B/D, 935-40 Bangbae- Dong, Seocho-Gu, Seoul Tel: (82) 2 521 6262.   Fax: (82) 2 521 5181

LEBANON: y.knot, Saifi Village, Mkhalissiya Street 162, Beirut Tel: (961) 1 992211   Fax: (961) 1 315553 Email: y.knot@cyberia.net.lb

LUXEMBOURG: Coats Benelux, Ring Oost 14A, Ninove, 9400, Belgium Tel: 054 318989 Email: sales.coatsninove@coats.com

MEXICO: Estambres Crochet SA de CV, Aaron Saenz 1891-7, Monterrey, NL 64650 Mexico Tel: +52 (81) 8335-3870

NEW ZEALAND: ACS New Zealand, 1 March Place, Belfast, Christchurch Tel: 64-3-323-6665 Fax: 64-3-323-6660

NORWAY: Coats Knappehuset AS, Pb 100 Ulset, 5873 Bergen Tel: (47) 55 53 93 00   Fax: (47) 55 53 93 93

SINGAPORE: Golden Dragon Store, 101 Upper Cross Street #02-51, People's Park Centre, Singapore 058357 Tel: (65) 6 5358454   Fax: (65) 6 2216278 Email: gdscraft@hotmail.com

SOUTH AFRICA: Arthur Bales PTY, PO Box 44644, Linden 2104 Tel: (27) 11 888 2401   Fax: (27) 11 782 6137

SPAIN: Oyambre, Pau Claris 145, 80009 Barcelona. Tel: (34) 670 011957   Fax: (34) 93 4872672 Email: oyambre@oyambreonline.com

Coats Fabra, Santa Adria 20, 08030 Barcelona Tel: 932908400   Fax: 932908409 Email: atencion.clientes@coats.com

SWEDEN: Coats Expotex AB, Division Craft, Box 297, 401 24 Goteborg Tel: (46) 33 720 79 00   Fax: 46 31 47 16 50

SWITZERLAND: Coats Stroppel AG, Stroppelstr.16 CH -5300 Turgi (AG) Tel: (41) 562981220   Fax: (41) 56 298 12 50

TAIWAN: Cactus Quality Co Ltd, P.O.Box 30 485, Taipei, Taiwan, R.O.C., Office: 7FL-2, No 140, Roosevelt Road, Sec 2, Taipei, Taiwan, R.O.C. Tel: 886-2-23656527   Fax: 886-2-23656503 Email: cqcl@m17.hinet.net

THAILAND: Global Wide Trading, 10 Lad Prao Soi 88, Bangkok 10310 Tel: 00 662 933 9019 Fax: 00 662 933 9110 Email: theneedleworld@yahoo.com

U.S.A.: Westminster Fibers Inc, 165 Ledge St, Nashua, NH03060 Tel: (1 603) 886 5041 / 5043   Fax: (1 603) 886 1056 Email: rowan@westminsterfibers.com

U.K: Rowan, Green Lane Mill, Holmfirth, West Yorkshire, England HD9 2DX Tel: +44 (0) 1484 681881   Fax: +44 (0) 1484 687920 Email: mail@knitrowan.com Web: www.knitrowan.com

For stockists in all other countries please contact Rowan for details

• Photographer: Moy Williams
• Stylist: Marie Wallin
• Hair & Make-up: Francis Prescott (One Photographic)
• Model: Joanna Stubbs (Select Models)
• Art Director: Marie Wallin
• Design Layout: Lee Wills

With special thanks to the following handknitters:
Jean Fletcher, Teresa Gogay, Betty Falconer, Pat Garden, Audrey Kidd, Susan Grimes, Yvonne Rawlinson,
Jenny Shore, Joyce Limon, Elizabeth Jones, Glennis Garnett, Judith Chamberlain & Arna Ronan.

First published in Great Britain in 2009 by Rowan Yarns Ltd, Green Lane Mill, Holmfirth, West Yorkshire, England, HD9 2DX
Internet: www.knitrowan.com
© Copyright Rowan 2009
British Library Cataloguing in Publication Data Rowan Yarns - The Milk Cotton Collection
ISBN 978-1-906007-59-1